An OPUS book

The First World War

Keith Robbins

The First World War

Oxford   New York

OXFORD UNIVERSITY PRESS

To John and Anne Thomson

Oxford University Press, Walton Street, Oxford OX2 6DP
Oxford New York Toronto
Delhi Bombay Calcutta Madras Karachi
Kuala Lumpur Singapore Hong Kong Tokyo
Nairobi Dar es Salaam Cape Town
Melbourne Auckland
and associated companies in
Beirut Berlin Ibadan Nicosia

Oxford is a trade mark of Oxford University Press

© *Keith Robbins 1984*

First published 1984
First issued as an Oxford University Press paperback 1985
Paperback reprinted 1985

British Library Cataloguing in Publiction Data
Robbins, Keith
The First World War.
1. World War, 1914–1918
I. Title
940.3   D521
ISBN 0–19–289149–9

Library of Congress Cataloging in Publication Data
Robbins, Keith.
The First World War.
(An OPUS book)
Bibliography: p.
Includes index.
1. World War, 1914–1918.   I. Title.   II. Series: OPUS.
[D521.R58 1985]   940.3   84–22622
ISBN 0–19–289149–9

Printed in Great Britain by
J. W. Arrowsmith Ltd, Bristol

Contents

List of Maps

Preface

This is not the first book on the First World War, though it is both one of the shortest and one of the most wide-ranging. It aims to provide a substantial narrative of the main military operations but also to assess many other aspects of the conflict. While it does not claim to be fully comprehensive, it does seek to introduce the reader to some of the social, psychological and political developments of these years which have been a particular feature of recent historical writing. The number of books on this war is vast and shows no sign of diminishing. The author has drawn gratefully upon this accumulated store of knowledge and wishes particularly to state his indebtedness to the authors whose books appear in the guide to further reading, even though no precise acknowledgement has been possible in a volume of this kind. He also wishes to thank his colleagues Dr D. R. Gillard and Dr E. Mawdsley for their helpful comments on an earlier draft, though naturally he retains responsibility for the final text. I am grateful to Miss Pat Ferguson for her exemplary typing.

K. G. R.

1 Entrances and Deaths

Most literate and intelligent men in Europe during the summer of 1914 considered that, in the circumstances, it was rather sensible to go to war. There was a mood of high excitement, even of exultation. War had come at last and the moment was to be savoured to the full. Freud declared that for the first time in thirty years he felt himself to be fully an Austrian. He was prepared to give the Habsburg empire another chance and allow it to become the focus for his emotional cravings. Ignotus, a Hungarian writer, felt that the war had to be: 'without it, we would have ended up like Turkey.' No worse fate could be conceived in the civilized apartments of Vienna or Budapest. The Czech writer Hašek naughtily records an Austrian officer commanding his mistress to embroider 'Gott strafe England' on her suspenders. Of course, his own hero, the good soldier Schweik, adopted a rather less energetic approach to the ensuing conflict. Austrian poets were elated by the thought that with every shot Germany was on the way to establishing mankind's 'golden empire on earth'. Whatever their notional political convictions, they had no doubt that with cold blood and hot iron 'wonderful work of man' was being done. Some of this martial zeal was of the kind that subsequently expressed itself in an eager search for unheroic employment in the imperial war archives; but not invariably so. And there were some, like Kafka, who could not, in any event, be spared from employment in a workman's accident insurance company.

Such enthusiasm might readily be explained by the peculiar circumstances of the Habsburg empire. Vienna, its capital, was a brilliant but febrile city, humming with presentiments of disaster, summed up by the writer Karl Kraus in the title of his book *Die letzten Tage der Menschheit* (The Last Days of Mankind). Immigration from different parts of the empire had produced or exacerbated existing social tensions. It was peculiarly difficult to operate parliamentary government, and there was little eagerness to attempt it. Czechs and Slovaks, Poles and Ukrainians, Croats and Serbs, were among the 'suppressed nationalities' jostling for position and satisfaction. Since the constitutional settlement of 1867, the Magyars had internal control within Hungary; friction between Vienna and Budapest was endemic and not without repercussions for the management of foreign policy. The future of these Habsburg domains, assembled over the centuries by marriage, purchase and conquest, was the subject of endless coffee-table speculation, but the subsequent demise of the monarchy should not necessarily encourage the notion that it was in fact on the point of collapse. The Habsburgs themselves were there to be criticized rather than replaced. Looked at as a whole, the empire presented a puzzling picture of industrial development and agricultural backwardness – regional contrasts were notable. 'Better a fearless end than endless fears' was becoming more than a cliché, particularly in military circles. The army took the view that it held the future in its hands. It could claim to be *the* embodiment of a state which could not rest its *raison d'être* upon national consciousness. The multiplicity of languages and the sus-ceptibilities they engendered frequently complicated organization and training, but senior officers could overcome these difficulties by their own linguistic proficiency. Conrad von Hötzendorf, chief of staff, claimed a fluency in seven languages – though perhaps over a restricted field of conversation. He was especially willing to quarrel in German – as he did, for example, with the heir to the throne, who resisted his suggestion that flautists in the military bands should be removed and trained as gunners.

Gunners, Conrad thought, might be useful against either the Italians or the Serbs, both independent states to the south with national minorities within the empire's boundaries. The temptation to act boldly was intermittently strong in Vienna, though it was recognized that the risks were great. In formally annexing Bosnia-Herzegovina in 1908, one demonstration of deter-mination had already been made. Populated by Serbs and Croats, and of mixed cultural and religious allegiance, this territory was a microcosm of the empire's problems. To annex a region in such a peremptory fashion seemed to show that Vienna intended to make no concessions to the aspirations of those who sought the inclusion of all Serbs in one Serb state, or, for that matter, to the aspirations of any other nationalities. Perhaps it also indicated that schemes for far-reaching constitutional change within the 'old' monarchy were also unlikely. The reactionary Archduke Franz Ferdinand occasionally dabbled with such plans and thus gained a liberal accolade.

It was to Bosnia that Franz Ferdinand took his morganatic wife in June 1914, partly to give her the kind of prominence that was only possible for her on the periphery. It happened that 28 June was the anniversary of the destruction of the Serbian army by the Ottoman Turks in 1389 and hence a day of heightened national emotions. The occasion proved too much for Gavrilo Princip, a Bosnian student, who killed the distinguished visitors, to the horror of the Bosnian crowd. *Mlada Bosnia* (Young Bosnia), with which Princip was associated, had little doubt that the assassination of Franz Ferdinand constituted 'tyrannicide for the common good'. The highest traditions of European thought were being distilled in the high schools of Bosnia and mingled with a more basic desire for blood. That the deed might have wider implications for Europe was not worthy of consideration. Though the activists were by no means united in their objectives and can even be accused of a nihilistic attitude towards the workers, there was a 'beauty' about the deed which was its justification in their eyes. They were merely the latest in a long line of fighters against alien oppression.

It was natural that the reaction in most European capitals was to hold the Serbian government in some way responsible for what had occurred. Effectively independent since the 1830s, Serbia had in that short time been handicapped in its development by some spectacularly bloody contests between aspirants to its throne. Serbian martial ardour, as displayed in the recently concluded Balkan wars, was undoubted, but somewhat primitive. It was not difficult to characterize Serbia as a peasant kingdom, an awkward appendage to civilized Europe. Although the full story can probably never be known, since there are crucial gaps in the evidence, it is most unlikely that the Serbian government directly instigated the assassinations. It did have some information that an assassination attempt might be made and tried, though only obliquely, to convey that intelligence to Vienna. Yet there were wheels within wheels, and there were deep quarrels and rivalries within Serbian political and military circles. It is not clear how all-embracing were the contacts of the secret 'Black Hand' organization. Formed in 1911, this society undertook the promotion of revolutionary activities in all territories inhabited by Serbs. It believed that the Pašić government was insufficiently zealous in liberating members of their nation enduring foreign rule. Its contacts and connexions extended deep into the army and administration of Serbia. However, the tracks that would reveal precisely what Princip intended and who may have supported him have been elaborately covered.

Old Emperor Franz Josef suddenly found himself in receipt of sympathy on the death of a much unloved nephew. Even in Western European capitals, murmurings about the plight of small nations took second place to the challenge to the established order which the assassination represented. The Serbian government, though not the Serbian press, tried to distance itself from the assassin and the 'Black Hand', well aware that impetuous circles in Vienna could find in the deaths the occasion for 'settling accounts'. There was, indeed, no lack of bellicose sentiment in the Austrian capital, though little clarity was evident, either about the kind of military expedition that might be mounted against Serbia or what its ultimate purpose might be. Looking back, it seems that an immediate punitive expedition might have been tolerated elsewhere in Europe. A swift response, however, was not something that came naturally in Vienna. Wise voices declared that it could not be assumed that the Serbian government was directly implicated. That aspect would have to be investigated, and if evidence of complicity was found the Austrian government would be placed in a strong position to take action with international approval. Many days passed without a firm decision. Nominally, control over foreign policy rested with Franz Josef, but old age in no way increased his capacity. Count Berchtold, his foreign minister, wanted the circumstances of the assassination investigated, though he shared Conrad's feeling that the time had come for action against Serbia. However, Tisza, the Hungarian prime minister, was more apprehensive. He feared that a successful action against Serbia might result in increased pressure on Budapest from Vienna. It is not surprising, therefore, that Berchtold considered it essential to take soundings in Berlin.

Germany and Austria-Hungary had been allies since 1879, and throughout the ensuing years Balkan issues had invariably posed problems for their relationship. Bismarck had been reluctant to become directly involved, but this reluctance was counterbalanced by the need to support the Austrians. It was a relationship which had become increasingly difficult to manage as the decades passed. Bismarck's successors had continued to regard the Dual Alliance as vital for German security, but there were occasions when Austria-Hungary could appear more of a liability than an asset. The interests of the two states were thus closely related but, necessarily, not identical. By the twentieth century, it was an alliance from which neither party could withdraw without throwing into confusion that network of alignments which, it was believed, gave security to Europe. If Vienna was not supported in the Balkans, that could only increase the scope for Russian activity in that area, and lead ultimately to the dissolution of the Habsburg empire. Nothing could alter the geopolitical realities of Central and south-eastern Europe. Such was the general diplomatic background when Kaiser Wilhelm and a motley collection of officials considered the letter from Vienna on 5 July. Bethmann Hollweg, the German chancellor, was empowered to give the Austrian ambassador a 'blank cheque'. The prevailing calculation seems to have been that Russia was not ready for war and also that the tsar would not want to appear to be condoning assassination. There would be strong words from St Petersburg, but no action. If Germany did not give backing to Vienna, Austrian prestige might be fatally undermined, with serious consequences for Germany herself. Support for Austria might also have the benefit of weakening the Franco-Russian alliance, for Paris, perhaps constrained by London, would urge the Russians not to intervene. To this end, it was best not to alarm the Western capitals unduly, and so Kaiser Wilhelm went ahead with his plans for his annual cruise off the coast of Norway. He predicted that there would be a period of tension for about three weeks, but then all would be well.

In fact, it was only after that interval that tension markedly increased. Embarrassed by the 'blank cheque', Vienna had been struggling to make up its own mind. The first results of the investigation into complicity by the Serbian government did not provide any very satisfactory basis for action. Tisza in particular became increasingly alarmed at talk of destroying Serbia. The Russians would certainly go to war rather than accept such an outcome. Would it not be better simply to achieve a clear diplomatic triumph by presenting some unpalatable terms to the Serbs which they would have little option but to accept? If they did not accept the terms at once then they could be persuaded to do so by mobilization. In any event, the Serbian government would have to be presented with a stiff document. Drafting took time, partly because no one was certain whether the purpose of the document was to make the terms acceptable or unacceptable. In the end, ten points were agreed but even then it was not until 23 July that a formal Note was sent to Serbia. The government was given forty-eight hours in which to reply to the demands, which included the cessation of all propaganda against Austria-Hungary, the arrest of certain individuals and the participation of Austrian representatives in investigations in Serbia itself. It was nearly a month after Franz Ferdinand's death: the moment when instant response might have been excused had already passed. The Serbian reply, qualified though it was, seemed to accept most of the requirements, though it was also accompanied by the mobilization of the armed forces.

The Russian reaction to these developments would prove crucial, but considerable mystery surrounded it. There was no doubt about the strength of pro-Serb feeling which existed in relevant circles in St Petersburg. For decades, Russian policy in the Balkans was composed both of 'Pan-Slav' sentiment, which loosely encouraged notions of rebellion against Ottoman rule, and a hard-headed appreciation that there was scope, in such circumstances, for the extension (not always welcomed by the supposed beneficiaries) of direct Russian influence. On the other hand, St Petersburg was not unaware of the dangers of a conflict which might expose the limitations of her ability to assist her putative clients. Russia was not anxious for direct confrontation with Austria-Hungary, her rival for hegemony over the Balkan peoples, at least not in the immediate aftermath of her defeat in the war with Japan at the beginning of the century. She had acquiesced in the Austrian annexation of Bosnia-Herzegovina. This inevitably gave the impression that Vienna was in the ascendant. It is not surprising, therefore, that it was widely held that Russian prestige would suffer if no support was now expressed for Serbia. In many respects, the Romanov empire was the mirror of the Habsburg – multinational, multilingual and extraordinarily diverse in social and economic development. There was the same tension between action and inaction – firm conduct might be catastrophic, or it might enhance the position of the throne. Foreign estimates of Russian strength showed comparable variation at this critical juncture. In Berlin, Bethmann Hollweg sadly reflected that there was no point in planting trees on his estate because it would be the Russians who would enjoy them. Pessimism of this order was catching. It rested on assumptions about the size of Russia, its population and accelerating, if erratic, industrial development. Whether these fears of future expansion explain or even excuse the mood in Berlin must remain an open question. Certainly, there was sufficient confidence in St Petersburg to make a strong line possible. The reaction of France might tip the balance.

France had been in alliance with Russia since 1894. It was an arrangement dictated by geography and France's defeat at the hands of Prussia in 1870–1, rather than the product of shared political systems or values. France was Europe's only major republic and the vaguely spiritual ethos of the Russian court could not present a greater contrast to the strident anticlericalism which underpinned successive French governments. Yet the two powers were held together by what they perceived to be their self-interest, and in mid-July the two most important Frenchmen, President Poincaré and Prime Minister/Foreign Minister Viviani were on an official visit to St Petersburg. In a champagne atmosphere even the *Marseillaise* was played. At a dinner in honour of Poincaré, the French ambassador found himself next to the wife of Grand Duke Nicholas (commander-in-chief and uncle of the tsar). She held out the intriguing prospect that the armies of the two countries would meet in Berlin after the defeat of the German forces; that she was the daughter of the ruler of Montenegro, the Balkan state adjoining Serbia, gave her prophecy particular urgency. Poincaré and Viviani undoubtedly talked to the tsar and his foreign minister, Sazonov, in less excited terms, though we do not know precisely what was said – but there is no reason to believe that Poincaré tried to calm the atmosphere. Both countries were agreed that Serbia could not be expected to acquiesce in Austrian interference in her own internal affairs, as required in the Note. The French party then sailed back to France. If war should come, France might recover Alsace-Lorraine – a prospect which pleased the many Frenchmen who had carefully nurtured their grievances.

Self-interest – most obviously, fear of German expansion – had brought the alliance into existence, and sustained it through some difficult episodes. It was a treaty which confirmed the appearance of confrontation in the relations between the major states of Europe. On the one side stood the Triple Alliance (for the Dual Alliance had been extended by the inclusion of Italy in 1882) and on the other the Franco-Russian Alliance. Such had been the pattern for two decades, though from time to time there had been stresses and strains within the alliances which reduced the strength displayed outwardly to the other side. Berlin, in particular, had made strenuous efforts to undermine the Franco-Russian alliance by trying to persuade some French opinion that a *rapprochement* with Germany would be advantageous. There were occasions, too, when a German–Russian arrangement had been contemplated by both sides. On the other hand, Italy had improved her relations with France and her status within the Triple Alliance was becoming uncertain. There had even been the possibility, during the Boer war, that the major European states might sink some of their differences and together exert pressure for concessions from the embattled British empire. It was in such a context that the British role now became steadily more important, though from a Central European perspective it was not easy to judge what course London would follow. To an extent, Britain stood outside the rival alliance systems. Her agreements with France (1904) and Russia (1907) related to quasi-colonial questions, chiefly on the fringe of Europe – in Egypt and Morocco, and in Persia. The implications of these agreements for European politics have been widely debated. Certainly, there were military conversations between Britain and France, but the British insisted that they retain a free hand. German attempts to weaken the Franco-British *entente* in 1906 and in 1911 over Morocco led to the opposite result. Yet there was never complete intimacy or understanding between London and Paris. The British Liberal government insisted that its policy in a crisis could only depend upon the precise circumstances. France was not given a blank cheque. Such uncertainty stemmed in part from the constraints imposed by Britain's global involvement. It also had its origins in the nature of cabinet government and foreign policy decision-making. When British statesmen stressed that they were circumscribed by public opinion (or at least by parliamentary opinion) this was not simply a dodge. While Sir Edward Grey was allowed (or created for himself) a certain latitude in the formulation of policy, a decision for war would have to gain the approval of the cabinet and carry the ruling party in parliament. Such approval could not be guaranteed in advance.

Quite apart from the Balkan crisis, the relationship between Britain and Germany was the most complex in Europe – at almost every conceivable layer of contact and communication. The early years of the Liberal government after 1906 had witnessed the 'naval' race between the two countries. A number of influential publicists in Britain appeared to have 'Germany on the Brain', and forecasts of impending conflict were frequent. On the other hand, Germany's somewhat imprecise claims for a 'place in the sun' – that is to say an increase in her share of the colonial spoils and a general position in world politics more consonant with her economic status – were received with some sympathy in Britain. Surely there was room for compromise and conciliation? Both schools of thought could be found in the Liberal party, and the foreign secretary had to take note. And by 1914 the view was sometimes expressed that in German–British relations the worst was past. This was partly because relations between Britain and Russia were not very harmonious. Russia showed little inclination to be strictly limited in her actions in Persia by the 1907 'spheres of influence' agreement with Britain. Suspicion of Russian intentions brought together in unlikely combination the 'India lobby' and Liberals critical of tsarist autocracy. Although there were some naval conversations between the two countries in May 1914, mistrust had not been removed. By the date of the Austrian ultimatum, therefore, British opinion appeared to be sharply divided. A. G. Gardiner, editor of the Liberal *Daily News*, was among those who rejected any notion of shedding blood for the tsar or for Serbia. Only by making it clear that the tsar would have to fight his own battles could Britain save Europe from war. The contrary position was that only by making it clear that Britain would not accept the destruction of Serbia would the Kaiser be deterred. But there was no consensus, either within the Liberal party, or indeed in politically alert circles in the country as a whole, on the source of the threat to peace. Given this division and the constitutional position, there is no need to invoke Grey's proclivity for fishing to explain his undramatic and ultimately ineffective actions. And if war did break out, there remained the question of whether Britain should join in.

The existence of these alliances and alignments among the Great Powers, and the ultimate failure of the 'Balance of Power' which, in theory, they were designed to sustain, has naturally prompted much discussion and debate. Why were the major states willing to contemplate war? A short answer is that the rivalries which characterized the European state-system in 1914 reflected an anxiety about survival which was all the more acute for being impossible to define with precision. It would be comforting if the rivalries could be located in certain specific conflicts of interest between individual states, but that is not easily done. It was the judgement of some contemporaries, most notably the British writer Norman Angell in his book *The Great Illusion*, which was widely discussed in the years just before 1914,

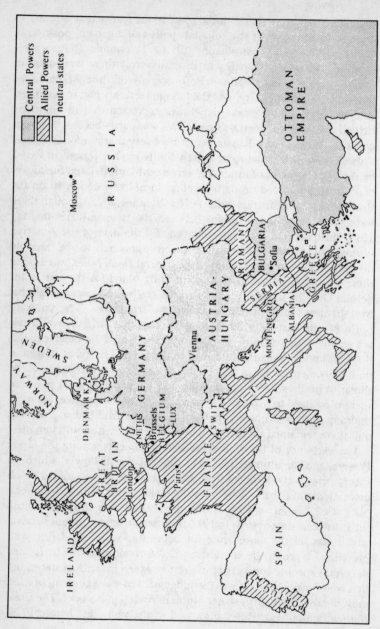

Central Powers

Allied Powers

neutral states

RUSSIA

Moscow

OTTOMAN EMPIRE

SWEDEN

NORWAY

GERMANY

DENMARK

ROMANIA

BULGARIA

Sofia

SERBIA

AUSTRIA-HUNGARY

MONTENEGRO

GREECE

Vienna

ALBANIA

I T A L Y

GREAT BRITAIN

NETHS

Brussels

BELGIUM

LUX

SWITZ

London

F R A N C E

Paris

IRELAND

SPAIN

1. Europe in 1914

that the costs of war would outweigh whatever advantages it might be thought likely to bring. The difficulty with Angell's theory, however, lies in the underlying assumption that policymakers were motivated by a straightforward calculation of economic or commercial benefit. Although a catalogue of 'factors making for conflict' could be almost infinitely extended, it must remain doubtful whether any of the rivalries that have been identified – involving North Africa, Alsace-Lorraine, Serbia, naval competition, to name but a few – in themselves 'caused' the conflict. It is not necessary to postulate a complex set of reasons simply because of the subsequent scale of the operations. An unanticipated event prompted the statesmen of Europe into taking actions which had long been contemplated but from which they had hitherto drawn back. It is, therefore, appropriate to think of the war as the climax to the late-nineteenth-century struggle for mastery in Europe – a phrase which reflects the aspirations of an era in its very imprecision.

In Serbia itself the public mood stiffened, though there were still some who preferred humiliation to death. The government decided that it could only accept the Austrian Note with some modification. Its resolve had been strengthened by Russian support – the meeting of the Russian council of ministers on 24 July had agreed to mobilize certain military districts, particularly those closest to Austria-Hungary. The Serbian ministers mobilized their army and a few hours later handed their reply to the Austrian minister in Belgrade. It was a masterly mixture of acceptance and rejection and Vienna did not know how to respond. On 26 July Grey suggested to Berlin that an international conference would be appropriate while, in the same quarter, Sazonov contemplated direct talks with Vienna. Meanwhile, both Austria-Hungary and Russia were taking steps which amounted to partial mobilization. While Vienna hesitated, the initiative rested with Bethmann Hollweg in Berlin but, although the risks in his policy were becoming hourly more apparent, he chose not to draw back. He could interpret Grey's suggestion of a conference as an indication that Britain did not wish to intervene – and the royal family network produced information allegedly to the same effect. Berlin put pressure on Vienna for a decision, indicating, in passing on the news of the British suggestion, that it would not be accepted. Of course, that is a shorthand statement. Politicians and soldiers were caught in a whirl of countervailing pressures. Steady nerves, supposedly the forte of Berlin, were not apparent, but the division of opinion was not a straightforward one between civilians and the military. In Vienna, for example, it was Berchtold, the foreign minister, who grew impatient with the military advice that more time was needed for an effective mobilization. In Germany, however, Bethmann Hollweg reeled under pressure from Moltke, who a little later took it upon himself to prod Conrad into action. In fact, Austria-Hungary did declare war on Serbia on 28 July, though nothing very dramatic happened immediately. The confusion of these days was not helped by the fact that both President Poincaré and Kaiser Wilhelm were, literally, at sea and Franz Josef was on holiday. It was not until the morning of 28 July when he was back in Potsdam that Wilhelm read the Serbian reply and pronounced that it removed every reason for war. He telegraphed to the tsar asking for help in smoothing over whatever difficulties might still arise. The tsar, meantime, had sent a telegram asking him to stop his allies from going too far. Neither 'all-powerful monarch' had his wish granted. It must be said, however, that even a monograph on the subject has failed to determine what Franz Josef thought he was doing.

Serious though it was, all that was happening was some inconclusive shelling by Habsburg ships on the Danube. It was not a European war, let alone a world war. The hope in Berlin was that Russia would still not intervene or that France would not support her. Paléologue, the French ambassador in St Petersburg, was doing his best to discount this latter possibility. The partial Russian mobilization proceeded and, it seems, was technically feasible, though a slower process than a general mobilization for which some of the Russian general staff pressed. If it continued, however, the likelihood of an Austrian general mobilization was inescapable. Also on 29 July, when the royal cousins were exchanging telegrams, Moltke warned that if that mobilization happened, it would be for Germany the *casus foederis*. Bethmann Hollweg had already warned the Kaiser that Russia had to be put 'ruthlessly' in the wrong. Moltke had little doubt that France would then intervene and, failing a miracle, a European war would occur. The only lingering uncertainty was the position of the British. Bethmann Hollweg told the British ambassador in Berlin on 29 July that Germany would not annex any French territory if Britain remained neutral. Grey thought that such a proposition could not for a moment be entertained – though that was his own opinion and not necessarily the cabinet's. The idea of mediation was still not dead. King George was mobilized in the small hours of

1 August to appeal directly to the tsar. By then, however, Nicholas had had two terrible days of nervous anxiety and worry. Late on 29 July, wishing to avoid responsibility for a monstrous slaughter, he had already reverted to the idea of a partial rather than a general mobilization. It was comforting, but probably illusory, to think that this decision made much difference and in any case he changed his mind again on the afternoon of 30 July. A few hours earlier, Moltke had unsuccessfully pressed Bethmann Hollweg to declare *drohende Kriegsgefahr*, the first stage of general mobilization. The chancellor still tried to urge patience on Berchtold, who was simultaneously being shown by Conrad a telegram from Moltke urging him to mobilize at once against Russia. The Austrian foreign minister asked, ahead of the historians: Who rules in Berlin? It was only a rhetorical question. When Moltke heard of Russian general mobilization on the morning of 31 July he successfully pressed for *Kriegsgefahr* and an ultimatum to St Petersburg. It expired unanswered in the evening on 1 August. Russia and Germany were at war. Austria-Hungary got round to a declaration of war against Russia five days later.

It was still theoretically conceivable that the war would not spread beyond Central and Eastern Europe. Already it was apparent that, despite her alliance with the Central Powers, Italy was not going to enter the war on their behalf. This neutrality would take some of the pressure off Austria's southern flank. But would France fight? French diplomacy in this crisis has been the least studied of all the major powers'. A paucity of materials makes commentary difficult, but it is hard to believe that in his repeated assurances of support in St Petersburg the French ambassador was exceeding the instructions of at least the president of France – whatever may have been the views of the French foreign office. On the afternoon of 30 July French forces were ordered close to but not on the border, and general mobilization followed at noon on 1 August. Even so, it was Germany that declared war on France two days later. Schlieffen, chief of the German general staff from 1891 to 1906, had bequeathed an imaginative, daring but perhaps foolhardy war plan. It was assumed that if Germany became involved in a war against Russia, France would support her eastern ally. Germany could not win a war on two fronts; therefore it was necessary to destroy France before (so it was imagined) Russia could effectively put her forces into the field. The weight of a Russian attack could then be resisted. The details of the plan had been subjected to some revision but its main thrust – which entailed a bold outflanking movement through Belgium and Luxemburg – remained intact. The first German troops were in Belgium before the ultimatum delivered to Brussels on 2 August had expired. King Albert in any case rejected the German demand for free passage and the surrender of his army. He was not impressed by the claim that French forces were advancing along the Meuse to Givet-Namur. He uttered an oath on receipt of a thoughtful letter from Kaiser Wilhelm reminding him that he was a German prince. Belgian troops engaged the enemy.

Major war on the continent was now inevitable, but Britain still trembled on the brink. Opinion in the cabinet and parliament remained fluid. On 31 July opponents of intervention in the cabinet seemed confident that war would not be sanctioned. Various groups inside and outside parliament mobilized in support of neutrality. The following day the prime minister privately confessed that his government was near the parting of the ways. Yet it is impossible to speak of clear-cut pro- and anti-war opinion. Sentiment varied from hour to hour as events unfolded. Grey was very firm, but only in the negative sense that he would resign if intervention was ruled out. A small group of ministers hinted that they would go if war were decided upon. In between stood a number of individuals of whom Lloyd George was the most important. When France was involved, all the arguments previously deployed in favour of the *entente* gained added force, though Grey accepted that no binding treaty commitment was involved. But if the issue had remained on the 'balance of power' level it must be doubtful whether a majority would have been obtained, or at least a big enough majority to sustain a continuing Liberal cabinet. It was the violation of Belgian neutrality which allowed Lloyd George and some others to find acceptable language with which to support an intervention of whose necessity they were probably already convinced. The knowledge that the Conservative leaders supported 'going in with France' perhaps helped to cement party solidarity. Burns and Morley, president of the local government board and lord president of the council respectively, who did resign, were not capable of causing serious political difficulty, and other more dynamic waverers came into line.

The British intervention was distinctive in several ways. Britain was the only country where there was serious argument at the highest level of decision-making about the merits of participation. There was linkage, if weak and ineffective, between well-placed opponents of intervention and some opinion in the country at large. Opponents of intervention, of course, were not necessarily opponents of war; neutrality could be urged on grounds of *realpolitik*. This argument, made possible by British constitutional arrangements, had no parallel elsewhere, not even in France to the same degree, and certainly not in Montenegro. Yet the degree of doubt was perhaps only a luxury of insularity, reflecting a confidence that in the short term invasion was unlikely. The corollary of this position was also that, as things stood, the British contribution was marginal and its effective weight would depend upon the nature and duration of the conflict. However, it was British involvement which from the outset did make the war global in scope. The repercussions, both in Africa and Asia, were immediate and of long-term significance.

Before the assassination of Franz Ferdinand, there were few observers who thought that by early August 1914 the major, and some minor, states of Europe would be in this condition. To observe that it was a state of affairs brought about by the alliances is a mere truism; the alliances now at the core of the conflict could be held to have preserved peace for twenty years. Naturally enough, there have been prolific attempts to explain, in some deeper sense, the sequence of events that has been sketched and to pinpoint responsibility. For some writers, big events need not have big causes. The play of the contingent and unintended together with the design and purpose of the leading actors produced a bewildering set of developments. If a telegram had arrived a little earlier, if the Russian minister to Serbia had not died of a heart attack at a critical moment (and so on) the outcome might have been different. Bethmann Hollweg, Pašić, Berchtold, Grey, Viviani and Sazonov all took risks which entailed, but did not necessarily intend, what followed. The summer of 1914 was not the first international crisis in Europe in the twentieth century, but previous episodes had been successfully 'managed', by luck or good judgement. The breakdown of 1914 was a breakdown. It does not even mean that the 'system' was fundamentally unsound. If that system is taken to be the 'Concert of Europe' – a set of rules, conventions and restraints informally agreed by a set of states within a given area existing in approximate equilibrium – then it had certainly been under strain since before the turn of the century. The events of 1914 finally disrupted that mutual confidence which was already badly frayed. Again, no single individual, cabinet, government or military staff may have planned such an outcome, though by specific acts they might have been able to prevent it. To speak of war by timetable is too simple, though the phrase rightly directs attention to technological and logistical developments, and the consequential planning machinery which constricted governments.

Any status quo – like that of Europe in 1914 – is only a status quo, which may imperfectly realize some yearned for but indiscernible just order. Whether the gains to be derived from 'grasping at world power' were worth the effort involved introduces quite other considerations. It was, of course, for diplomacy to facilitate the adjustment of power relations and, in this more restricted sense, the advent of war did illustrate the shortcomings of its practitioners. One by one, the ambassadors wept and departed to their home countries. There were 'three cheers for Count Mensdorff' as the Austrian ambassador left his London station. Sir Edward Goschen, British ambassador in Berlin, sadly left the German capital, well aware that it would be some time before he stayed in his favourite home again, in Carinthia, within the Habsburg empire. Who was to blame for this ambassadorial distress must remain a matter of emphasis and perhaps, as those who do not read diplomatic documents assume, lies beyond the realms of telegrams and despatches. One newspaper editor may have reached the heart of the matter. Alcide de Gasperi, prime minister of Italy after the Second World War, but then a citizen of the Habsburg monarchy, wrote at the time that he declined to offer any comment on the origins of the war. It was in the hands of God.

If the diplomats trailed lugubriously home, many poets were exultant. Productivity reached unparalleled heights in the belligerent countries, though perhaps the record was held in Germany and German-speaking Austria. It has been estimated that one and a half million war poems were written in August 1914 – 50,000 a day. Poets were indeed active but it is worth recalling that some soldiers went through the entire war without meeting one. Despite Sassoon and Graves, that was even possible in the Royal Welch Fusiliers. Of course, the literary traditions of individual countries shaped the language and imagery of particular writers, but certain common themes do emerge. Almost universally, there was a sense of excitement and release from Rupert Brooke's world 'grown old and cold and weary'. He rejected the world of the bank clerk and conventional commercial routines (not that he had ever experienced them), leaping as a swimmer into 'cleanness'. And for many, it was the prospect of fighting (rather than simply becoming a soldier) which held promise. Carl Zuckmayer, a German writer, had felt gloomy before 1914 at the prospect of his compulsory military service with the restriction and subordination it entailed. Now the army represented liberation from bourgeois narrowness and pettiness. It relieved him (and many of his young contemporaries) from worrying about the profession his parents expected him to follow. War contrasted with that stuffy and petrified world. Death could well lie at the end of the road but was only 'the worst friend and enemy'. In early August, German and French poets expressed their joy at leaving home, though they were fully aware that they might be killed within the month. For many of them there was an apocalyptic and transcendental dimension to what was impending. Millenarian themes found acceptance in surprising quarters. Even 'respectable' publishers were keen to disclose that soothsayers in the seventeenth century had foretold the wickedness of Kaiser Wilhelm II.

Yet it may not be wise to take literary testimonies as the authentic guide to the mind and mood of Europe. The educated middle class from which most writers sprang had a psycho-social perspective which need not be universalized. Nevertheless, in the major cities of Europe, men and women of different social classes (as indicated by their dress) flocked into the streets in celebration. The crowds outside Buckingham Palace did chant 'We want war' on August Bank Holiday. This apparently 'natural' and spontaneous solidarity was not the result of any objective unsettling of social order and class distinction but was more analogous to a carnival or fête involving a temporary suspension of social behaviour and an indulgence in unproductive expenditure. The world was in a gorgeous state of flux and the railway station became the nodal point of existence. Of course, the picture must not be pressed too far and the excitement may have been an essentially urban phenomenon. Becker's detailed investigation of French public opinion discloses a much more complex picture than might be suspected from immersion in the stanzas of war. On the basis of prefectorial reports, he suggests that news of mobilization was received in markedly different spirit in different parts of the country. The word 'enthusiasm' was used sparingly. Sentiment was most favourable south of the Loire and, perhaps significantly, enthusiasm was conspicuous in the Basses-

and Hautes-Pyrénées – furthest away from the impending conflict.

From Serbia to Scotland, patriotism provided the rallying cry. In Toulouse, café orchestras interrupted their programmes to play the *Marseillaise* to which the crowds responded with 'Vive la France!' In Pau a *manifestation patriotique* went on all night. Comparable events took place on a gratifying if not immense scale throughout Europe. *La Patrie* or *der Vaterland* could draw on a powerful emotion. But if national sentiment was very evident, the exuberance of its expression was as much an indication of its fragility as of inherent strength. While a 'nationalist revival' can be detected, with reverberations in clerical, academic and military circles, its strength and depth should not be exaggerated. Xenophobia did not characterize French intellectual life. There was no particular hostility towards Germans in areas like the north-west where some worked and lived. Even within Alsace-Lorraine itself, there was no unalloyed desire to return to France. The most emphatic assertions of the importance of restoration came from Alsatian 'exiles' in Paris. Throughout the country, there remained hundreds of thousands of peasants who possessed only a dim awareness of the fact that they were Frenchmen. So with imperial Germany which, despite formal unification, remained constitutionally, culturally and religiously divided. Solidarity was an aspiration rather than a reality. Frequently, too, the most strident expressions of patriotism came from those whose own status might otherwise be thought dubious. The author of the celebrated 'Hymn of hate against England', so popular in Germany, was a Jew whose own contribution to victory was limited to the wartime editing of the *Carpathian News*.

The United Kingdom too was not without its problem of nationality. English poets did not apostrophize the 'United Kingdom of Great Britain and Ireland' but 'England'. They gave St George a new lease of life, conjuring up a lyrical picture, not of course of Liverpool, but of leafy lanes and green fields. Wyn Griffith, however, talked Welsh to men in his regiment as a way of reaffirming the wholesomeness of rural life as opposed to the urban, industrial world where English ruled. Above all, a sense of divided loyalty was to be found in Ireland, and nowhere more poignantly expressed than by W. B. Yeats in 'An Irish Airman foresees his Death'. Flitting between London and Galway himself, he wrote:

> Those that I fight I do not hate,
> Those that I guard I do not love;
> My country is Kiltartan Cross . . .

'Kiltartan Cross' could be a Slovak village in the Tatra mountains, or indeed anywhere in the peasant world of Eastern and Central Europe. Austria-Hungary and Russia could not even pretend to evoke undivided national sentiment – loyalty and integrity had perforce to find what embodiment it could in throne and altar. For millions, it was all a strange business. An English nurse told a group of Russian soldiers in early 1915 that she was from an ally of their mother country. They might have been more impressed if they had ever heard of 'Angliya' or known where it was. Yet even in the more sophisticated (because more literate) urban islands, 'nationality' was a precarious concept, as 'nationalists' were to find.

If poets praised the prospect, they had little notion of what war would be like. The last war between two major European powers had been between France and Prussia. Although casualties had been comparatively heavy, the conflict had lasted merely months. Since then French troops had only taken part in limited engagements in Africa and Asia. The Serbs had very recent experience fighting alongside and then against the Bulgarians. The Russians were just beginning to recover morale and confidence from their defeat by Japan a decade earlier. The British had spent a decade trying to work out the implications of their exhausting conflict with the Afrikaners, hitherto not ranked highly amongst the world's military powers. The Italians had just had a difficult war in Libya, though only a little one, with a yield of Italian dead disappointingly small for Corradini, Marinetti and other Italian exponents of heroic warfare. Austria-Hungary had not been involved in war since the reconstitution of the state as a dual monarchy in 1867. German forces had only seen very minor service outside Europe since the formation of the empire.

That record seemed to suggest that wars might be nasty and brutish but they would be short – months rather than years. This 'short war illusion' was widespread in military and political circles. Its popular expression was the notion that the war would be over by Christmas. From a naval standpoint, Admiral Beatty thought that the timing of the war could have been a lot worse. He told his wife that the navy would be able to fit its battles in and have the whole thing over before the long winter nights came on. The French writer Jules Isaac subsequently recollected that his predominant feeling was to get the war 'over and done with'. This sentiment can be found in many other sources in all the belligerent countries. If the risks politicians took in the July crisis are thought unacceptable, their behaviour might at least be explained by suggesting that their conception of war was very different from what turned out to be the reality. Yet not everybody shared the view that the war would be over quickly with a minimum of disruption and destruction. There was the warning provided by the grim casualties of the American Civil War half a century earlier. These matters were naturally discussed in the staff colleges and war academies of the continent and the possibility of a gruellingly lengthy war could not be eliminated. Moltke himself, a few days before the declaration of war, wrote that it would have such devastating consequences that it would take Europe at least a decade to recover from it. In Britain Kitchener (likened by Lloyd George to a lighthouse occasionally emitting illumination only to be followed by darkness) also felt that it was wrong to anticipate a swift conclusion. Other soldiers and politicians were so guarded in their observations that it is impossible to tell what they really felt.

Speculation about a future war was not confined to professionals. The Polish-Jewish financier Ivan Bloch wrote a massive work, *The Future of War*, which was translated from Russian into the other major European languages and widely discussed in the decade before the war. His stress upon the gravity of war in an evolving industrial society was deeply disturbing. H. G. Wells in a variety of writings showed an uncanny perception of what war might be like. Plays and novels raised the spectre of the invasion and a certain spy fever developed. The moral was plain – be prepared. Friedrich von Bernhardi's *Deutschland und der nächste Krieg* (Germany and the Next War) had a similar message for Germany – and his volume, published in 1912, was rapidly reprinted. These 'voices prophesying war' helped to create a climate of expectancy which perhaps fostered the very event that was being predicted.

So, at least, 'pacifists' thought. Peace societies existed in all the major European countries and claimed to be growing in strength and influence. However, despite the international congresses that were held – it was reputedly at the Glasgow conference in 1901 that the word 'pacifist' was coined – there existed a wide variety of viewpoints about the best way to establish the common goal of peace. One emphasis was upon arbitration as a means of settling disputes between sovereign states, but there was no unanimity about the best machinery for this purpose or how judicial decisions could be implemented if the parties concerned would not accept them. In some countries (France, for instance) positivist and legal emphases were most prominent in peace circles, while in others (Britain, for example) Christian and moral imperatives remained paramount. Judged by the level of activity, the peace movement was strongest in Britain and weakest in Germany and Russia. This disparity caused a problem. It was only too easy for German critics of pacifism to draw attention to its apparent acceptability in Britain. Of course the British wished to preserve a peace which served their interests and the high moral tone they adopted only disguised their self-interest, or so it was claimed.

It was also possible for writers who accepted that peace was to be preferred to war to disagree with some of the central assumptions of the peace movement. Most pacifists tended to assume that the international system would evolve in such a way that the role of force would progressively diminish. Power would either cease to be important or would be non-military in character. The German historian Hans Delbrück was among students of international politics in the major countries who saw little ground for this assumption. There were political antagonisms which could not be eliminated and which would cause states to continue to fight. Pursuit of the balance of power still offered the best chance of avoiding war. Each state held the other in check by means of the subtle and sensitive system of alliances. He further argued that reduction in the level of armaments would not make any significant contribution to the prospects of peace. On the contrary, governments might be more tempted to run the risk of war if the forces involved appeared likely to be small. If Europe increasingly had the appearance of an 'armed camp', that augured well for peace.

In 1914, the pretensions of the international peace movement were ruthlessly exposed. Pacifists were not especially quick to perceive the implications of Franz Ferdinand's assassination. The leading German peace journal, for example, devoted much more space to the death of another Austrian, Baroness von Suttner, author of a celebrated book, *Lay Down Your Arms*. A gathering of European peace societies took place in Brussels on 30 July, but to no avail. It was already apparent that the leading pacifists of Germany and France took the view that pacifists should not cease to be patriots. German pacifists turned out to be stridently confident that their country was fighting in self-defence. Only in Britain did a significant number of those who had been active in pacifist circles remain opposed to

British intervention in the conflict. Even here, however, the amalgam of sentiment which went under the name of 'peace movement' swiftly dissolved, to leave only a small residue of those who had an objection on religious or moral grounds to participating in warfare. Most of those who did now support the war could not, of course, do so on humdrum grounds. The German pacifist Fried talked optimistically about war being the continuation of pacifism's work, only by other means. Likewise, in Britain, war was seen among many of its supporters as a judgement on the existing 'international anarchy' and the prelude to a more effective system of international government. It was but a short step to 'war to end war'.

Church leaders, too, had little difficulty in bestowing their blessing upon the conflict. In England, there was no lack of confidence that the nation had been divinely commissioned to end Prussian militarism. One clergyman declared international treaties to be 'God's demand notes, endorsed by His Divine hand'; to disregard them entailed eternal damnation. The chaplain general, an authority on death, interviewed potential chaplains with great care. His advice on the preparation of the wounded for death was so comprehensive that some feared *rigor mortis* might set in before the instruction could be completed. In Berlin, Reinhold Seeberg, a celebrated theologian, pronounced that the slaying of the unworthy was an act of charity. His Baltic origins enabled him to detect a considerable number of such individuals both to Germany's east and west. In August 1914, a special chant was intoned in Russian Orthodox churches: 'Most Gracious Lord, crush the enemy before our feet!'. The wonder-working ikon of the Mother of God, painted on a board from the coffin of St Sergii, was sent from its monastic home to the front by imperial command. A Russian victory near Lvov and the Allied success at the Marne were reported shortly afterwards. In Austria-Hungary, chaplains showed exemplary zeal in stressing loyalty to the emperor. French Catholics showed, in many cases, a greater desire to die for the Third Republic than they had to live under it. The ease with which a holy war could be declared should not disguise the fact, however, that many theologians and ordinary Christians were acutely aware of the conflicting claims of their consciences. Tolstoyans in Russia and many Quakers in Britain felt themselves unable to bear arms and adventist groups in all belligerent countries doubted whether what was taking place was really Armageddon. Despite the secularization of the European mind, it was still a recognizably Christian Europe which was at war. Indian Sikhs and Moroccan Muslims were to stare uncomprehendingly at the shattered Calvaries they encountered in battle. The testimony of many soldiers confirms that holy communion on the field of battle was a most moving experience. Transfiguration remained a possibility amidst the destruction.

Until a few years before 1914 it had still been common for the German socialist paper *Vorwärts* to pour scorn upon the dreamers of perpetual peace to be found among the bourgeoisie and in some church circles. Only socialists correctly diagnosed the causes of war and, in the International, had an instrument which could prevent it. The memory of the extraordinary socialist Congress of Basle hastily summoned in November 1912 was still strong. Governments were reminded by speakers from all the major European countries that proletarians regarded it as a crime to shoot each other for the profit of capitalists. But it was left unclear how resistance was to be mobilized and what degree of class collaboration for this purpose could be tolerated. The idea of a general strike jostled uneasily with an emphasis on improving relations between Britain, France and Germany. Even supposing that a greater co-ordination of effort would have been possible, no specific likelihood of war was identified in the ensuing eighteen months. Electoral progress was evident in a number of countries and confidence in socialist strength was growing as preparations were made for the next international congress, to be held in August 1914. Like the peace congress scheduled for that year, Vienna was the appointed venue; neither meeting took place. Socialist leaders – Kautsky, Bernstein, Ebert, Scheidemann and Adler – showed as much zeal for foreign holidays in July as did their monarchs. Only very late in the month did the gravity of the crisis strike them. The hastily convened meeting in Brussels failed to agree on either a course of action or the cause of the war. Divisions within and between national parties sprouted rapidly, being brought to the surface in circumstances where the rhetoric which had previously disguised them no longer served. A Dutch socialist had conceded in July that national feeling was stronger than anything else. The working class had not managed to destroy the spirit of belligerency and would fall into line once the guns spoke. With certain exceptions, that proved to be the case throughout Europe. German socialists voted for war-credits and French socialists supported the idea of a national partnership – the *union sacrée*. There was, perhaps, only one consolation; war might precipitate revolution and, paradoxically for men who had condemned war so vigorously from the platform, it might have more chance of success if the war became protracted.

Thus, when it came to the point, there was scarcely a social group in Europe which could not hope to derive some benefit from the war even if, in their own eyes at least, it was being imposed on them by another. The old élites, it has been claimed, unrestrained by the bourgeoisie, systematically prepared their drive for retrogression. Yet it was this aristocratic order which contrived to retain some semblance of supranational sentiment. During the crisis, 'Willy' and 'Nicky' corresponded in English. Yet, to survive, the old order had to appeal to a more blatant national sentiment – one which found a ready response both among the middle and working classes. *Dulce et decorum est pro patria mori* was the appropriate epitaph for the early fallen; no alternative loyalty could withstand its appeal.

The scale of the struggle that began in 1914 surprised most observers. As the months and years passed, the only description that seemed appropriate was simply the 'Great War'. Only with the outbreak of a second struggle in 1939 did it become the first of two world wars. Some historians have preferred the earlier term, arguing that it was not really a 'world' war. It was, like the first couple of years of the 1939 conflict, a European struggle. There is certainly nothing to be gained from suggesting, at this juncture, that the outcome of the war was determined in the Yellow Sea or the South Atlantic – though significant encounters did take place there. Dismissing such alternatives, however, does not immediately disclose the true epicentre of the conflict or highlight where precisely the war was won. It is believed that the first 'British' shot of the entire war was fired by a Gold Coast sergeant. Each major belligerent, inevitably, had a different perspective on the fighting. The theatre in which its forces were chiefly engaged frequently assumed decisive significance and dominated subsequent historiography. To this day, the myths and realities of national experience set the framework and determine the historical priorities. For some, the kernel remains Flanders fields – the historian has a duty to struggle once more through that muddied landscape if he wants to understand what the war was about and what it was like. For others, the fighting in north-east Europe occupies the centre of attention and becomes normative. Strangely, too, the labels habitually used in the English-speaking world take

Germany as the reference point. In fact, of course, British troops had to move east to fight on the Western front. For most Frenchmen, the war was taking place in the north of their country. British politicians and soldiers talked about the Eastern front, although for their Russian ally it was a war being fought in the west and south-west. The Scandinavian states (and The Netherlands) were all neutral, though not unaffected. The Southern front was difficult to categorize: initially, Vienna had only to face the forces of Serbia but had a more formidable opponent in Italy after the summer of 1915. Ottoman Turkey, after initial wavering, came into the war in October 1914 on the side of the Central Powers. Only recently defeated in the Balkan wars, Constantinople faced possible assault from Greece and Bulgaria, from Russia to the north and feared further erosion of her control over large areas of the Arab world from the British based in India and Egypt. Switzerland apart, therefore, the war was eventually to involve every European state from the Atlantic to the Caucasus. Only countries in the south (Spain and Greece – to some degree) and the north kept out of the fighting.

The extent of such involvement necessarily entailed a wide divergence in the terrain of battle. It is difficult, in such circumstances, to speak of 'typical conditions' for warfare, and wrong to suppose that precisely the same military problems confronted commanders in Belgium and the Balkans. A perspective which focused on the war in northern France would lead to the impression that the war soon became quite static, while concentration on the Eastern front would lead to the opposite conclusion. In a more general sense, too, the number of belligerents increased the diversity and complexity of objectives. The smaller countries, like Bulgaria and Romania, entering the war in October 1915 and August 1916 respectively, were balancing, in the event not very successfully, their assessment of local advantage and the overall position of the respective sides. The conflict between Austria and Italy can be seen as the final phase in a sequence of nineteenth-century battles. Within the continental struggle were individual wars which had a momentum and intensity of their own and whose outcome was of more immediate significance than the outcome of the general war. On the other hand, individual battles were often decided by the general balance of men and resources open to the opposing combinations. To use the word combination, however, may overstate the position. Germany, Austria-Hungary, Ottoman Turkey and Bulgaria hardly presented a natural grouping from almost any standpoint – particularly since the latter two had but recently fought each other. It was difficult to conceive, and certainly impossible to execute, a common strategy involving mutually beneficial reinforcement. There was no doubt that Germany was the dominant partner. Such clear superiority served simultaneously to remind Germany's leaders of the burden which they carried and at the same time to release them from the sometimes intractable problems of joint formulation of strategy and policy. Of course, German high-handedness offended Austrian sensibilities but there was little that Vienna could do, since such treatment reflected military and political realities.

The position of the Allies was more complicated. Britain, France and Russia could all claim parity of status and perhaps of power. Although they all agreed to fight together and, at the outset, not to conclude a separate peace, distance in itself made effective collaboration between the Western Powers and Russia very difficult. The suspicion that Russia might in fact reach a separate agreement with Germany never completely died. Tension between London and Paris initially arose out of the disparity in the size of their armed forces. Neither government was in theory prepared to accept subordination to the other or to plan an effective joint operation from the start. In practice, in the battles on French soil, the British frequently did have to take second place. Although the disparity diminished as the war proceeded, when it began they only fought in a small section of the front and with only a small army. Inevitably, too, when the war was taking place in France it was the French whose emotions were most involved. The detailed consequences will be pursued in subsequent chapters; it is sufficient to remember that at all levels linguistic difficulties impeded a united effort.

Such petty problems existed alongside deeper disagreements and fears. Paris suspected that the British addiction to the 'indirect approach', a belief that punishing blows could be struck against Germany by amphibious assault or in some distant theatre, stemmed from an unwillingness to accept that the Western front was the vital struggle, on which all effort should be lavished. Although both countries were imperial powers, the British empire was the more diverse and far-flung. The British colonies of settlement were not near at hand (in contrast to the French settlement in Algeria), but in Australia, New Zealand, South Africa and Canada. Sentiment and, except in the case of Canada, the prospect of territorial gain brought them into the war at Britain's side in 1914, although in South Africa and Canada there had been opposition from some Afrikaans and French speakers respectively. Behind the assertions of loyalty to the mother country, however, lay a somewhat prickly national self-consciousness. It was convenient for the newly unified countries of Australia and South Africa that German colonies (New Guinea and South West Africa) were close at hand and ripe for conquest. Expeditions to this end (and against German colonies elsewhere in Africa) necessarily gave the war an extra-European dimension. In time, too, conquest raised questions about the ultimate future of these territories. This issue was to demonstrate that the conquerors were not mere agents of the 'imperial government' in London, but it could at first appear that the war was only non-European in so far as it involved the miscellany of German colonial possessions.

That impression was misleading in at least two aspects. The involvement of Ottoman Turkey automatically extended the scope of war in the Near East. That in turn raised the sensitive issue of Arab aspirations and the extent to which they should be encouraged. To enlist their support might entail a comprehensive redrawing of the map and the formal establishment of European authority. And the bland phrase 'European authority' only disguises the fact that Britain and France had in the past been rivals for influence in the area and would be so again. Even the Italians were to anticipate a stake in the future disposition of Turkey itself. The complications were potentially enormous, but unless some Arab support was enlisted (or so it was believed), the defeat of the Ottoman empire would prove a laborious and expensive business. As it was, the British expected that the burden of fighting, at any rate in the valley of the Euphrates, would be carried by Indian troops. India had automatically come into the war at its outset and the government of India found the response gratifying. There were some nationalist protests about the lack of consultation but their impact was slight. Princes proved generous with their purses. But the entry of Turkey caused justified concern – the viceroy describing the Muslims as 'undoubtedly sulky'. A careful watch was kept on Pan-Islamic propaganda in Urdu. Strategic arrests kept the agitation under control and, with small exceptions, the Indian army remained loyal to the Raj. Even so, the ripples of the war in the Near East extended throughout the subcontinent.

The involvement of Japan was the second reason why the non-European aspects of the war cannot simply be regarded as the conquest of German possessions. Britain had allied with Japan in 1902 and, after revision, the alliance remained intact in 1914. The Japanese navy would be useful against the German Pacific fleet. But there was hesitation in London about the extent to which such assistance was to be encouraged. Japan would expect some *quid pro quo*, and Australia and New Zealand feared the expansion of Japanese influence in the South Pacific. British intelligence officers in India were also apprehensive (with less justice than they supposed) that subversion there would have the support of Japan. It therefore seemed desirable not to encourage Japanese offers of help. On the other hand, if Japan were cold-shouldered, there was a danger that her pressure on China might increase.

Limited though it was, the war in South-East Asia impinged on the United States, ruler since 1898 of the Philippines. Washington was also deeply interested in the triangular relationship between Britain, China and Japan and the implications for its own Asian position. European powers, however, chiefly thought about the United States in an Atlantic context. The initial neutrality of the United States came as no surprise in London, Paris or Berlin. There was little expectation that this status would change but what seemed of vital importance was to make it as benevolent as possible. Britain and Germany, in particular, devoted themselves to explaining their respective positions in the most favourable light. Even though, subsequently, the Germans believed that the British had shown unexpected skill in their efforts, the British were in the most difficult position. Many in public life found it hard to accept that President Wilson could not distinguish between right and wrong, and resented the even-handed approach adopted by the White House. It was scarcely credible that this detachment was genuinely disinterested. It was feared that the United States would take over markets Britain was temporarily unable to supply – particularly in South America. Such attitudes encouraged a disregard of American sensibilities about the 'Freedom of the Seas'. On the other hand, there was considerable 'English-speaking' sentiment, a desire not to upset American opinion and a sometimes undisguised hope that circumstances would change and the British empire and the United States would actually fight side by side. If there was something special about the relationship between Britain and the United States there was a fairly general recognition in diplomatic circles that, in one way or another, the American people might determine the outcome of the European war. The ramifications of the war were global from the outset, even if the connexions between the various battles were not yet discernible to contemporaries.

2 Land Warfare

1914

Despite the forecasts made by some strategists, the war was not over
by Christmas 1914. It had appeared, for a time, that the British and
French were going to be defeated in northern France and Belgium,
with a similar fate awaiting the Germans on their Eastern front and
the Serbs on their northern front, but in all cases the defenders had
averted disaster. The fortunes of the Habsburg forces fluctuated, but
they too had not been completely routed. For the moment, at any
rate, the attackers had lost the upper hand and could not sustain their
impetus. The ambitious initial plans of the commanders were in
ruins and everybody had to begin again.

The German Schlieffen plan, named after a former chief of the
general staff between 1891 and 1906, had been predicated on the
assumption of a two-front war. Rapid mobilization would enable
Germany to defeat one enemy and then turn upon the other. Since it
was assumed that France would mobilize more quickly than Russia,
that concentrated assault would have to be in the west. The French
would not be able to retreat far, at least not without losing their
capital city. France could only be knocked out in six weeks by an
outflanking movement – which would entail the invasion of
Belgium. Speed of assault and numerical superiority would bring
success.

The general drift of the plan was known in Paris but no precise
precautions were taken against it. The French had their own
elaborate Plan 17 and they too would take the offensive without
tarrying for anyone. The right would attack Lorraine while the left
held a German army moving through Belgium. An *offensive à
outrance* sounded splendid, though the anticipated disparity of
numbers was disturbing. The action (or inaction) of the Belgian army
was a matter for speculation. The action (or inaction) of the British
army came into a similar category. Even supposing an expeditionary

force landed, the Germans derived some amusement from the notion that they would promptly 'arrest' it. The prospect of giving the British a thrashing was a wish communicated by the Kaiser to his Maker.

The Belgian forts and garrisons put up a spirited defence against the German First Army which attacked Liège – arguably the most strongly defended city in Europe. Even so, they did not prevent Ludendorff, then a staff officer, from obtaining the surrender of the citadel by appearing before it in nothing more frightening than a motor car. The forts were then smashed systematically by Skoda howitzers and all resistance came to an end on 16 August. German troops spilled into Belgium in large numbers, but their ultimate destination was unclear. Rapid marching enabled the infantry to cover nearly 200 miles in a fortnight. Brussels fell on 20 August. King Albert and his men, busy blowing up bridges, railway lines and tunnels, retreated to Antwerp, there to await the arrival of Winston Churchill. Lacking serious opposition, the Germans had to make do with burning such university libraries or shooting such priests or English nurses as they encountered *en route*. If the enormity of such acts could be magnified, British propaganda made every attempt to do so. The schedule of advance slipped a little, though the fact that the British Expeditionary Force had landed was not thought a major obstacle to success.

The French were not idle. One cavalry corps came near to Liège but could not even find any Germans. In a display of *élan*, elements of the French First Army captured Mulhouse on 9 August. It was an achievement made possible by the absence of German troops; they returned the following day, and the French retreated across the frontier. More serious adventures took place in Lorraine, beginning on 14 August, when almost a third of the entire French army was committed. The Germans initially retreated – as was envisaged in their own planning – but on 20 August they stood and fought, inflicting heavy casualties in the ensuing week. Individual French units fought heroically but, underestimating the bulk of the opposing forces, the offensive had undeniably failed. The recapture of Alsace-Lorraine would clearly have to attend the deepening crisis in the north. The unexpected strength of the Germans on the French right led to the misleading supposition that they could not be as strong on the left as some feared. The French Fifth Army on the left was, however, nearly panic-stricken; their condition was not

FINLAND

Petrograd

LATVIA   • Riga

LITHUANIA

Danzig

GERMANY   E. PRUSSIA
            MASURIAN
Tannenberg LAKES   • Grodno R. Niemen

Posen   RUSSIA

            POLAND

Breslau   R. Warta • Warsaw

                    Brest-
                    Litovsk

                              R. Bug

                                        PRIPET MARSHES

            • Cracow
R. Vistula
        • Gorlice • Lemberg
        Przemyśl

CARPATHIAN MOUNTAINS

AUSTRIA-HUNGARY   R. Dniester

━━━━━ Deepest Russian penetration
▭▭▭▭ Deepest Austro-
       German penetration   ROMANIA
─·─·─ State boundaries 1914
▰▰▰▶ German offensives 1915
━━━▶ German offensives 1918
▨▨▨▶ Russian offensives 1914
▨▨▨▶ Russian offensives 1916

            0   200   400 km
            ├────────┼──────────┤
            0   200 miles

2. The Eastern Front

relieved by the appearance of the BEF near Mons. However, even without the angelic assistance which some discerned there the British riflemen gave a good account of themselves when von Kluck's forces launched a frontal attack. In due course, however, the British position could be turned by a flanking movement. Dispirited, the French commander in the region decided to retreat and did not trouble to inform the British of his departure. Retreat was the general pattern and there were signs of alarm in Paris. A French directive of 24 August talked of holding the line from Amiens to Verdun, but on the left additional strongpoints were being conceded. The British were heavily engaged at Le Cateau.

The Germans were now in a quandary. Certainly, in the last few days of August, they encountered unexpectedly fierce resistance, but they had little doubt that they had put the British to flight and had the French Fifth Army in their grasp. There was an obvious temptation to abandon the idea of encircling Paris and instead to encircle the Fifth Army. This would have the advantage of closing the gap between the two German armies of von Kluck and von Bülow, but by going east of Paris von Kluck's flank would be exposed. The British, meanwhile, expressed an interest in 'refitting' on the Channel coast, and it took the personal intervention of Kitchener, secretary of state for war, to reassure the darkly suspicious French that this would not happen. The French government left Paris on 2 September, but the city's commander declared his determination to fight to the bitter end. Helped by confusion among the German commanders in the early days of September, the French now contemplated a counter-strike, using the Sixth Army stationed east of Paris. From 6 September onwards other armies, including, at a leisurely pace, the British, moved northwards. In the confused sequence of battles that followed over the next few days, which collectively go under the name of the battle of the Marne, the British and French undoubtedly achieved a major success. A simultaneous attempt on the part of the Germans to take Verdun failed, and they carried out a general withdrawal from Nancy to the Vesle. Yet they were not pursued very vigorously, and the line stabilized. Casualties had been heavy – as much as 40 per cent in some places. The Allied munitions supplies were running short. The British contribution had perhaps proved crucial – von Kluck subsequently declared that they had prevented him from taking Paris.

Over the next couple of months, the focus of military activity shifted to the area between the river Oise and the coast – sometimes grandly described as the 'race to the sea'. Commanders on both sides attempted, in a series of actions, to turn the other's flank. Fierce but inconclusive fighting took place in late September and early October in this sector. At the other end of the line, further German attempts to outflank Verdun failed, but they did capture St Mihiel and a section of the west bank of the Meuse before they were stopped. In the north, a sustained German attack in early October led to the surrender of Antwerp on 10 October. Not even the presence of Winston Churchill and a few thousand British marines could prevent the inevitable. Churchill, King Albert and the Belgian army extricated themselves in time. The Belgians joined the British in Flanders and, together with a small French contribution, they formed a not invariably solid line confronting the Germans. The Germans appeared confident that they could reach the Channel ports, though the British also appeared confident that they could attack. The Allies did give ground in the series of battles which took place between mid-October and mid-November known collectively as the first battle of Ypres, but the Germans did not achieve their objectives. Even the momentary presence of the Kaiser failed to accomplish a breakthrough. It was at this point that the 'Western front' stabilized in a line extending from the coast at Dixmude to the Swiss border. On both sides, commanders talked of striking successes to be achieved in the following spring, but there was to be very little variation in the line for three years.

During these months, the war in Eastern Europe followed a not dissimilar pattern. The Germans feared a lengthy two-front war, and so the French looked for relief from their Russian ally. There had been some planning for this contingency – the Russians were to attack on the fifteenth day of mobilization. It was thought imperative to maintain such a timetable if the Schlieffen plan was to be defeated. East Prussia was the obvious target for an offensive and it could be attacked by two Russian armies moving north and west. However, co-ordination between them did not prove easy and the first, under Rennenkampf, moved into East Prussia on 17 August, two days ahead of the Second Army under Samsonov. Their chances should have been good since the German force at the disposal of Prittwitz was smaller than either Russian army. The numerical inferiority of the Germans, whose objective would be to avoid fighting both armies simultaneously, was balanced by the fact that the terrain offered considerable advantages for defenders. The Germans hastily moved

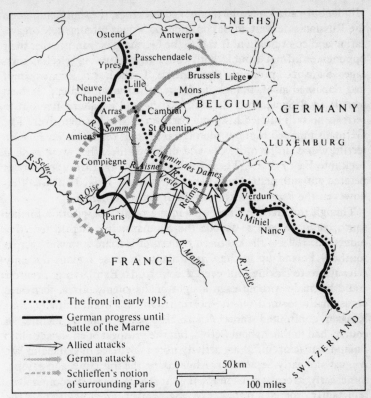

The front in early 1915.

German progress until
battle of the Marne

Allied attacks

German attacks

Schlieffen's notion
of surrounding Paris

0   50 km

0   100 miles

3. The Western front

mobile guns from some of their fortresses and had control of the railway lines to give them flexibility. Even so, after a minor setback, the
first success went to the Russians at the battle of Gumbinnen on
20 August. Prittwitz wanted to abandon East Prussia and even had
doubts about being able to hold the line of the Vistula. Such timor-
ousness led to his replacement by the formidable combination of
Hindenburg and Ludendorff a few days later. They had no intention
of retreating and instead elaborated plans which had already been
made by a member of Prittwitz's staff. The decision was taken to
tackle the Russian Second Army by moving troops down to the south
but this defensive withdrawal was not initially seen as the prelude to
the spectacular encounter of 29 August. In the battle of Tannenberg
the Russians lost 100,000 men prisoner and many guns. Although

Hindenburg and Ludendorff emerged as heroes, the shortcomings on the Russian side were most conspicuous – poor intelligence, organization and co-ordination. It was to the Germans' advantage that their opponents did not trouble with codes when sending wireless messages. Samsonov promptly shot himself. To the north, Rennenkampf had remained aloof, though he did repulse the subsequent German assault on 8 September. Sensing that he had no alternative but to retreat, he skilfully led his army back across the Niemen river. The Germans pursued him but soon ran into stout resistance on Russian territory and, in turn, by the end of September, they were pushed back into East Prussia. These battles in the land of lakes and forests petered out with neither side in the ascendancy. Judged by casualties, however, the Russians had lost substantially more men.

Though the Germans had won in the north, the position further south could be said to favour the Russians. But such a tentative judgement reflects the confused pattern of warfare sprawling across southern Poland up to the Carpathians. In these regions not only railways were lacking, but even decent roads. Exhilarating progress could be made without even a sight of the enemy. Great fortresses occasionally loomed on the horizon. On this front, initially, four Russian confronted three Austro-Hungarian armies. Vienna, of course, had to think about Serbia, but the prospect of an advance into Poland was tempting. Vast activity now took place in Galicia in late August and early September. After taking the initiative, and gaining some early successes, Conrad, the Austro-Hungarian commander, reluctantly ordered a retreat on 11 September, intending to hold the line of the river San. The Russian numerical superiority seemed to be decisive and the Habsburg forces gave further ground and appealed for German assistance. Ludendorff and Hindenburg now turned their attention to this front. A German push gave rise to the suggestion in mid-October that Warsaw would be captured. This was an exaggeration and by the end of the month the German army concerned was virtually back where it started. There were further offensives in November, with particularly heavy fighting around the town of Lodz, but neither side could claim undisputed advantage. The fortress of Przemyśl, on which the Austrians placed great store, was blockaded and the prospect of its fall caused Vienna to quake. Trenches and fixed lines even made an appearance in this theatre where bewildering movement had hitherto been prevalent.

At the end of the year, Austria-Hungary could not even claim to have destroyed Serbia. The Habsburg armies had invaded from the north and west of the country in mid-August and, after making initial progress, they were soon driven back across the border by the Serbian army – largely composed of Balkan war veterans. Potiorek, the Habsburg commander, launched a second invasion on 8 September, but a week later he had come to a halt. This time, however, his forces were not expelled from the country. The Serbian commander, Putnik, withdrew his forces to higher ground and waited for the next attack, which came on 5 November. He had evacuated Belgrade and the prospect of defeat seemed imminent; but, on the contrary, in early December he was victorious. Potiorek ordered a retreat and Austrian forces once more crossed the border on 15 December. The fighting on this front had been particularly fierce. The Serbs exploited their knowledge of the terrain to the full. Preoccupied by the precarious situation in Galicia, the Austrians decided not to mount a further attack for the time being.

Further east, too, there was activity. At the end of December, some two months after Russia and Turkey had declared war, a major encounter took place between the two armies near Kars. The Russians defeated a larger Turkish army and, for the time being, thwarted the Turkish objective of fomenting a Pan-Turanian uprising in the region. In the south, Turkish garrisons in Syria were reinforced and the British did the same in Egypt. They also formally annexed Cyprus. In Mesopotamia they were more adventurous. From the outbreak of the war, the India office had been particularly concerned about the oil installations of the Anglo-Persian company at Abadan. An expedition reached Bahrein at the end of October and proceeded to capture the town of Basra on 22 November, striking north in the following month. Running up the Union Jack in such a region seemed a good idea, but British and Indian troops too easily underestimated their opponents.

Military activity elsewhere in the world was slight. The Germans surrendered their fortress at Tsingtao in China in November to the unlikely combination of the South Wales Borderers, Indians, and Japanese forces. German Togoland fell to the West African Rifles in August and the Australians and New Zealanders successfully accepted a British invitation to occupy German New Guinea and German Samoa respectively. The Afrikaner rebellion inside South Africa unfortunately delayed the anticipated assault on German South West Africa. The invading force designed to capture German

East Africa had to retreat, in embarrassing haste, to its ships. The combined might of the British, French and Belgian forces aiming to incorporate the German Cameroons seemed to disappear into the jungle and little was heard from them. It became necessary to look to the British West Indies Regiment for advice and assistance in such conditions.

Taking the conflict as a whole, a general stalemate seemed to be emerging. There was a relationship between the various fronts but it was a stabilizing rather than a winning connexion. The Russian operations had forced the Germans to take troops from the west and, though to a degree that can never be precisely established, had thus helped to achieve the Franco-British victory on the Marne. On the other hand, the Germans appeared to have successfully stiffened Austro-Hungarian resistance at a point when that, too, had appeared on the verge of collapse. Both sides had averted defeat. Could either achieve victory?

1915

On Christmas Day 1914 there was a ceasefire in France. British and German soldiers took the opportunity to have a game of football, but the season of goodwill proved short-lived. Firing began again on the following day. The year 1915 was one of adjustment on all sides. Soldiers and civilians began to appreciate that the war might last a very long time. Casualties had been incurred on a scale that entailed the restructuring of entire armies. Fresh thought, too, had to be given to the logistics of a conflict which was taking a very different course from what most theorists had assumed. A new balance would have to be struck between the need for fighting men and the requirements of domestic industry. If the problems appeared formidable, very few wanted actually to stop fighting. Victory still seemed a feasible and legitimate objective, whatever the cost in human life or material destruction. No army was so demoralized that it could not envisage future success – given the necessary reorganization and re-equipment. Even so, 1915 witnessed a vigorous debate, in all capitals, about where these successes were going to be gained.

In London, there was no lack of suggestions. On Boxing Day 1914 Hankey, its secretary, circulated a paper to the war council in which he described the 'deadlock' in the western theatre of the war as 'remarkable'. When more troops became available, was it not time to consider using British seapower to open a new front, perhaps directly against Turkey or through the Balkans on Austria-Hungary? Admiral Fisher had a yearning to descend in force upon Sleswig but was unsuccessful in persuading others to share this desire. Among the politicians, Lloyd George and Churchill both wanted something new. The former argued on New Year's Day 1915 that only signs of a 'clear definite victory' would satisfy the public that sacrifices were not in vain and persuade neutral states to throw in their lot with the Allies. Churchill saw a naval assault on the Dardanelles as a way of achieving these objectives. In mid-January, after a less than exhaustive scrutiny of the implications, the war council agreed that preparations for such an expedition should be made. It seemed that the following month the Gallipoli peninsula could be taken and the way would be open to Constantinople. Turkey could be knocked out of the war, Russia supplied with munitions and neutral Balkan states would be so impressed that they would join the Allies at once. It was difficult to believe that a few prominently placed Turkish shore batteries would stand in the way of these accomplishments, even granted that the warships to be employed were mostly elderly and the naval commander was ailing. Advocates of this adventure conceded that the Western front still existed and might yet prove decisive but argued that a sideshow could not do any harm. But cold feet did not exist only in the trenches. Alarmed that his newest 15-inch-gun fast battleship, the *Queen Elizabeth*, was to be committed, Fisher wanted 'quietly to enjoy' the advantage brought by possession of a powerful fleet. He did not want that quiet enjoyment spoiled by operations that 'could not improve the position'. Kitchener's enthusiasm for the project did not extend to promising military support. What carried the day, in the end, was a general, if inarticulate feeling that this was the kind of enterprise which the British knew how to handle, coupled with the belief that Turkey could not be taken very seriously as an opponent.

In Paris, the perspective was rather different. There the looming German presence on French soil was an inescapable reality. Military commanders still placed their faith in the possibilities of attack. Disliking bulges, Joffre had his eye on the so-called Noyon and St Mihiel salients. Preparations were made for a major offensive in Champagne in mid-February. However, even in France, the idea of an alternative front had some support – Galliéni also chose New Year's Day as the occasion to offer politicians a new perspective. It was not enthusiastically taken up and French collaboration in the Dardanelles affair was as much the product of a desire to restrict British ambitions as to defeat Turkey. The exuberance of the French minister of the marine may have stemmed from direct experience of Churchill's verbosity. Such a conversion may explain his conceal-ment of the plans from his cabinet colleagues. Behaviour of this kind did not improve the auguries for the expedition.

In Berlin, too, choices had to be made, though in this instance more directly between an eastern and a western offensive. In the heart of Europe Falkenhayn, the German minister of war, who had also replaced Moltke as chief of the general staff, took the view that a decisive blow in the West was still possible. He advocated the careful husbanding of men and *matériel*. Fresh troops and fresh supplies could be welded into a central reserve whose concentrated might could overwhelm the Allies. Such a project could sound convincing, but, at least in terms of prestige, those who had been concerned in the 'failure' in the West contrasted it with the position of those who had achieved 'success' in the East. Hindenburg and Ludendorff lost no opportunity to point out that total victory could be achieved in the East if they were given the necessary resources. Falkenhayn was not convinced, arguing that a victory in the East achieved only at the cost of weakening the position in the West was short-sighted. One alterna-tive canvassed was to stop eastern operations altogether and possibly reach an agreement with the tsar for a separate peace. On the other hand, there was no firm evidence that the tsar would detach himself from his Allies. Falkenhayn remained committed to an attack in the West, even though he did not have as many troops as he felt necessary, but circumstances seemed to give a campaign in the East priority. There was constant pressure for assistance from Vienna – a demand that would grow if Italy entered the war. Likewise, Turkey might become more vulnerable and require help. Dithering, at this level and to this degree, had unfortunate repercussions for Germany. It was not clear whether the objective was to cripple Russia and provide an opportunity for a major attack in the West or whether Russia could actually be knocked out of the war by a major German offensive.

In St Petersburg, a kind of hope survived but here too there were conflicting opinions. Some maintained that in the south-west the Habsburg forces were only clinging on precariously. The fortress of Przemyśl would fall and the Magyars would sue for a separate peace – a sequence which would have beneficial results in the

Balkans. More troops on this front would allow the momentum to be continued. A contrary view held that it was the German position in East Prussia which constantly handicapped Russian operations in the central sector. Admittedly, in prevailing circumstances, a drive straight through to Berlin was unlikely but the constant threat of being outflanked could be removed by an attack into East Prussia from the south. There was something to be said for both arguments and the rival generals did more than speak, they acted. They preserved their own strengths and made sure that Russian forces were divided rather than concentrated on one objective. Just to complicate the position further, there was a good deal of excited talk about Russian claims on Constantinople.

In Vienna, the military situation in the north-east produced paradoxical reactions. Conrad pressed the case for German assistance but claimed that his forces were capable of taking the offensive. It is difficult to tell whether he deceived himself or had become very excited because of his close collaboration with Hindenburg and Ludendorff against Falkenhayn. His standard reply to criticism was to confirm his detailed knowledge of the Carpathians. However, whatever configuration of German–Austrian collaboration emerged in the north, events in the south could pose equally grave threats. The prospect of Italian intervention became imminent. In Rome, the German government attempted to keep Italy neutral by holding out the prospect of territorial compensation at the expense of Austria-Hungary – over 800,000 Italians lived within the frontiers of the monarchy. Vienna did not directly participate in these discussions, almost preferring the prospect of a war with Italy to the possibility of making concessions. Meanwhile, the Italian government carefully considered the various bids it had received, though in an atmosphere of mounting public controversy. In such circumstances, Vienna could not withdraw forces from the Italian frontier to fight elsewhere. The Serbian successes in December 1914 also vexed the Austrians. Unfortunately for Vienna, manpower could not be spared for a counter-attack, and the two armies simply faced each other across the Danube. The calm was only disturbed by the strange developments which occurred when the familiar river launches tried to behave like torpedo boats. For their part, the Serbs were suffering severely from various epidemics and the casualties sustained in their heroic efforts over the previous months. Observers were not sanguine about their chances when fighting was resumed on any scale – but that in turn might well depend on what happened elsewhere in the Balkans and on the fate of the British naval bombardment in the Dardanelles.

The Allied warships attacked on 19 February (a small number of French ships were also involved) and their gunfire did have some initial success in silencing the forts at the entrance to the straits. Bad weather then held up the assault for days, but when it resumed the reports were favourable. However, newly laid mines in the straits caused much alarm thereafter. De Robeck, who replaced the sick Carden as commander, launched a major new battleship assault on 18 March. Its progress has been variously interpreted: much play has been made with the fact that it subsequently emerged that Turkish ammunition was running short and thus a breakthrough might have been possible if the attack had been pressed. But de Robeck decided to stop. British east coast trawlermen, hopefully described as 'minesweepers', did not prove adept at catching mines. Despite hasty improvisation, time passed and the Turks, marshalled by the German general Liman von Sanders, were able to bring in fresh supplies and troops. It might have been prudent to abandon the operation at this juncture, but that was not the general reaction.

British, Australian, New Zealand and French troops were also now in the vicinity under the command of Sir Ian Hamilton. A general who was also a poet might be an asset amongst the islands of Homer. It had originally been envisaged that the British regular division at his disposal would garrison Constantinople. A more immediate objective now seemed to be the Gallipoli Peninsula, but even that immediacy was relative. Hamilton went back to Egypt to work out a plan and find some maps. Putting men and equipment ashore in a hurry was not something which had been envisaged and it took time to find lots of little boats. It hardly came as a surprise to the Turks when, on 25 April, the landings actually began. Beaching the old tramp steamer the *River Clyde* seemed a good idea, until it transpired that troops trying to get ashore were directly in the line of Turkish fire. Heroism and confusion abounded – something which Hamilton could not resolve from his position on the *Queen Elizabeth*. Allied troops could not, or would not, advance off the beaches, but neither could they be dislodged. That seemed to be the position by mid-May, but it had been gained at a heavy price. An invading force of 70,000 had sustained casualties of 20,000 and the medical services could not cope. There were explosions at home too. Feeling that hell was freezing over, Lord Fisher resigned as first sea lord in protest at the conduct of operations. He hoped to preserve his beloved *Queen Elizabeth* from the German submarines he suspected to be in the area. The Liberal government was also a casualty – being replaced by a coalition in which Churchill no longer had a place. Even so, more British divisions were sent and unsuccessful attempts were made to break out of the beachheads over the next couple of months. Since two beachheads had proved unsuccessful, to open up a third was an obvious step. Guessing the whereabouts of the opponents was of the essence in these operations and secrecy was vital. Nevertheless, the ignorance of the commanders on the spot of each other's intentions was excessive. Stopford, who led the landing at Suvla Bay on 7 August, brought experience gained from being Lieutenant of the Tower of London to the task. His men stayed by the shore and only tried to move inland when it became inappropriate to do so. Over the next fortnight, bitter fighting took place but all that could be claimed was that there existed three beachheads where there had been two. Hamilton was replaced in October, but the troops remained. Kitchener himself went out to survey the increasingly cold scene, concluding that withdrawal was inevitable. The departure of 35,000 men from Suvla Bay and Anzac Cove on 18 and 19 December was the best organized feature of the campaign. It was matched by the evacuation of Cape Helles in early January. Allied casualties were in the region of 200,000 and so were those of the Turks, but the Allies had nothing to show for their efforts. The Turks, frequently dismissed as a military factor after the Balkan wars, had shown that they could repulse the European invader. General Liman von Sanders did not underestimate his role, but at Suvla the credit undoubtedly went to the Turkish commander, Mustafa Kemal.

Gallipoli was a fiasco, but it possessed an enduring fascination. In its wake reputations crumbled and some of them never recovered. Individuals tried to explain their actions, but the biggest lesson was the hardest to learn – an expedition of such a character required meticulous planning from the outset if it was to have any chance of success. The great British amphibious exploit was improvised throughout. Inevitably, the repercussions of failure spread throughout the Balkans. At the beginning of the year, forcing of the Dardanelles had been seen as part of a strategy which was to set the Balkans alight in the Allied cause. Bulgaria was courted both by the British and the Germans. After months of vacillation, King Ferdinand plumped for the Central Powers who seemed in the ascendancy. In turn, Venizelos, prime minister of Greece, showed an anxiety to involve his country on the Allied side. Anxious to counterbalance the mainly British enterprise in the Dardanelles, the French quickly agreed to supply a substantial number of troops under a commander, Sarrail, whom it was politically expedient to remove from France. Unfortunately for the Allies, while these moves were afoot, Venizelos was forced to resign. The Allies went ahead none the less and installed themselves in Salonika (a seaport only recently returned to Greek hands). Greek political opinion was bitterly divided by their presence. The general crisis was imminent since Austrian and German armies started to move over the Danube and Sava rivers on 7 October. It was Falkenhayn who had taken this decision two months earlier, arguing that the removal of the Serbian obstacle would enable supplies to reach Turkey – on whose effective participation he placed increasing hopes. It was assumed that the Bulgarians would advance from the east and cut the lines to Salonika. They would gain Macedonia as a reward. The Serbian army would be trapped in the mountains in winter and destroyed. Mackensen, who commanded the Austro-German forces, had planned his campaign thoroughly and Belgrade fell in two days. The Serbian commander retreated in a south-easterly direction when it became apparent that the Bulgarians could both prevent his forces reaching Salonika and prevent Sarrail's forces materially assisting him. The French did have some short-lived successes but they could not prevent Mackensen engulfing Serbia. However, he did not destroy the Serbian army on its own soil. An epic national evacuation now took place. Battling against the elements and (at times) the Albanians, they struggled across the high mountains to the coast in late November and December. Monarch and men went forth together, with no certainty that either would escape disaster. If a tragedy for the Serb nation, the year brought the expectations of the Allies in the Balkans crashing to the ground. They only retained a dubiously legal foothold in Salonika from which they might, at some stage, make a new beginning.

The Turkish success at Gallipoli also revived British fears about internal security in India and the reliability of Indian troops serving abroad. The viceroy of India, Lord Hardinge, took the view in 1915 that with a show of sympathy and some 'very moderate but justifiable concessions' India would remain peaceful. In fact, a succession of ill-fated plots against British rule occurred throughout the year. Franz von Papen, then military attaché to the German embassy in

Washington, spent some time organizing a plot to invade Burma by German-officered Sikhs from the jungles of north-western Thailand. It did not succeed. However, it was not upon such episodes that public attention focused. Rather was there a thrill of pride at the progress of British and Indian forces in Mesopotamia. The original purpose of safeguarding the oilfields of southern Persia had been achieved with so little difficulty that the temptation to proceed further up the valley of the Tigris proved irresistible. In the commons in early November the British prime minister spoke in moving terms of the need 'generally to maintain the authority of our Flag in the East'. Three weeks later, British forces were defeated at Ctesiphon, some twenty miles from Baghdad. Particularly since the capture of Baghdad had been thought imminent, it was difficult to grasp that British and Indian forces had sustained another defeat at the hands of Turkey. Townsend, their commander, withdrew to the small town of Kut with Turkish troops in pursuit. In early December, he supposed that it would only be two or three weeks before the siege would be lifted with the arrival of additional troops from India or France. For the moment, it seemed that even in Mesopotamia the Ottoman empire could defeat the British.

Against these setbacks on the southern or Mediterranean front of the war, the Allies could only derive a modest consolation from the fact that Italy had at last, in May, joined the struggle. The debate inside Italy had been protracted and characteristically tortuous. In the end, the interventionists carried the day because the Entente Powers had been able to be generous in their offer of territory, mainly Austrian territory. Indeed, it was only against Austria-Hungary that Italy declared war – it was not until August 1916 that Germany became an enemy. The Treaty of London, signed on 26 April in secret, would be certain at a peace settlement to bring Italy into conflict with South Slav aspirations along the Adriatic but for the moment these were put on one side. It was claimed that only with Italian assistance could the Allies win. The actual declaration of war placed the Italian army in some difficulty. The Italian chief of staff had died of a heart attack two days after the assassination at Sarajevo. His successor, Cadorna, wanted to place in readiness all the Italian units which would be bound for the French frontier or to assist Germany on the Rhine. When that turned out to be the war which would not be fought he had to transfer men and materials to the north-east. The serious obstacle was that, for the most part, the

Italian boundary lay beneath the line of mountains – a natural barrier which was also fortified. The frontier was nearly 500 miles long and posed many problems. The Trentino jutted into northern Italy and could give the Austrians the opportunity to strike at Venice. This opportunity was more apparent than real because it was difficult to supply a major army through this region. Even so, the Italians could only contemplate defensive operations in the north-west. In the centre it did not seem sensible for anyone to suggest fighting in rarefied altitudes. Only in the north-east might the Italians advance by striking across the Isonzo river with the objective of reaching Trieste. Cadorna helpfully explained to the Italian senate in April 1915 that he would be there within a month. At that stage, too, it had been possible to envisage linking up with the Russians and Serbs in a grand triumph in the south-east of Europe. However, strategists were fond of pointing out that the Isonzo front presented certain difficulties. The crossings were exposed to mountain batteries – which could not be silenced until the river had been crossed. And by the time that the first offensives were launched, in June 1915, co-ordination with Serb forces was impossible. Between June and December there were no less than four offensives on the Isonzo, with short intermissions to re-equip. The Italians captured prisoners and equipment but their casualties were heavier than those of their opponents – over 250,000. Against a well-armed and well-positioned enemy the bravery of the Italian infantry availed little. G. M. Trevelyan, the English historian of *Risorgimento* Italy was there, serving in a British Red Cross ambulance unit. Cholera raged in the trenches and he reported suffering soldiers crying out 'Viva la guerra' in bitter mockery and cursing those who had drawn Italy in. Even a little touch of King Victor Emmanuel in the night could not console his soldiers for the fact that such losses had only brought trifling additions of territory.

The failure of the Italian and Near Eastern campaigns came as a great disappointment to those who had hoped that they would provide a short cut to victory. The emphasis inevitably returned to the theatres where the war began. Of course, the peripheral proceedings had not entirely occupied the stage. The French repeatedly stressed the need to concentrate upon the enemy at the gates. The reconquest of occupied territory, particularly since it contained so much of French heavy industry, was an understandable preoccupation. Nor was advance out of the question. Early in the New Year

(1915) and through into the spring fresh British (and some Canadian) troops crossed the Channel. The British Expeditionary Force was divided into two armies under Haig and Smith-Dorrien. It was generally calculated that the Allied armies comfortably outnumbered the German. Somewhat apprehensive about events in Eastern Europe, Joffre argued that it was time to strike before that disparity in numbers was wiped out. There were also other factors at work. The British and French commanders took particular care not to appear to be co-operating and in the encounters that took place over the next few months seemed anxious to score points at each other's expense. In addition, Sir John French, the commander of the BEF, was afraid that Kitchener (who, besides making a striking poster, spoke disturbingly excellent French) might think of some alternative use for the new troops with which he was being supplied, and make an arrangement behind his back. However, no alternative deployment was devised, and on 10 March the British began a heavy artillery bombardment in front of the village of Neuve Chapelle. British and Indian infantry then captured what remained of it and found themselves momentarily having 'broken through'. This achievement was disorientating and the surprise was not pressed home. German reinforcements arrived and French brought the advance to a halt on 13 March, having acquired some 400 acres. The French attacks in Champagne, which had started in mid-February, came to an end six weeks later with scarcely greater success. Allied casualties in both engagements came to around 100,000. At such a rate of advance, it would take a long time to clear the Germans from French soil.

It was the German turn next. No major offensive was contemplated in the West but it was necessary to encourage the belief that an offensive capacity remained – the reality was that troops were being transferred to the East. The installation of cylinders in the front-line trenches from which gas-clouds could be discharged seemed to meet the need of the hour. They were released on 22 April on a section of the Ypres salient held by French Colonial, Canadian and British troops. It happened to be Moroccans who were enveloped by chlorine gas. Their discipline had never been exemplary – it now ceased to exist. The British and Canadians put up a brave fight on their exposed flank, but it became clear that the gas did not only affect North Africans. Soldiers died from suffocation in gas-filled trenches. In the fighting, the Allies lost a two-mile zone to the north and east of

Ypres. It was decided, none the less, that this reduced salient was worth retaining – a decision which was to have bloody consequences in the future. However, the Germans too were surprised by the apparent success of their new weapon and likewise lacked the reserves to hand to exploit the Allied discomfort. French dropped Smith-Dorrien and replaced him by Plumer – who promptly carried out the withdrawal which his predecessor had been criticized for undertaking. Fighting continued spasmodically in early May but this second 'battle of Ypres' can be said to have come to an end with the failure of a German assault on 24/25 May. Crude respirators proved marginally more effective in assisting the defenders than the wet handkerchiefs initially employed. Even so, the murky yellow fields gave a new quality to death in battle.

Meanwhile Joffre had launched the attack he had long contemplated but had delayed because of the events at Neuve Chapelle and Ypres. The country in which the campaigning was taking place was all relatively flat, making the 'ridges' of considerable importance. On 9 May, in Artois, the French Tenth Army launched an attack against Vimy ridge with considerable *élan*. A foothold on the crest of the ridge was secured, but then, in very heavy fighting, the French were beaten back – defeated by the intricate trench networks which the Germans had established and by their skilful machine-gun emplacements. There were fresh assaults, culminating in particularly bloody engagements in mid-June, but at the close the Germans were still in control of Vimy ridge. The French suffered some 100,000 losses and the Germans 75,000. The British role in this fighting (as opposed to the Ypres struggle when some 60,000 men had been lost) was intentionally subsidiary. On 9 May, after heavy bombardment, Haig and the First Army attacked with the objective of taking the Aubers ridge, near Festubert. It halted on the same day. Further attacks were pressed later in the month on the pleas of the French, but scant progress was made. The obliging way in which British troops went 'over the top' directly on to their guns surprised the Germans. The machine-guns kept firing, but the British did not.

This dismal record explains the British interest in alternative theatres of conflict. In early July, British and French ministers met in France to assess the picture. It was then agreed that a fresh effort should be made at Gallipoli and if that did not succeed then there would be a further western offensive in the autumn: meanwhile, it turned out to be a pleasant summer in northern France, only marred by somewhat routine trench warfare. It was disturbed by the offensive in September. The plan this time was for a simultaneous offensive to be launched by the British and French in Artois and the French in Champagne. Joffre, who masterminded the operations, declared that the attack should take place at Loos, a potential battlefield replete with slag heaps and coal mines – particularly favourable ground, in his view. French and Haig dissented but were overruled by Kitchener, who urged that everything possible should be done to assist the French, even though the losses would be very heavy. There was the encouragement that gas could be used against the Germans, though a fickle wind was to ensure that they would not be the only victims. The offensives in neither sector surprised the Germans, who had reinforcements available. However, Scottish troops made good progress at Loos – perhaps they were at home among coalfields – and looked round for reserves to sustain their advance. Haig had none available. French held them too far back and was dilatory in producing them: an element of jealousy may have been involved. When the tired reserves did arrive they ran immediately into a German counter-attack which pushed them back. Thrust and counter-thrust in a conventional manner continued until early November when the line stabilized. The British had advanced about two miles. Further south, meanwhile, Foch, commanding the French Tenth Army, launched a further attack on Vimy ridge, but although progress was once again made it could not be sustained. The assault was soon abandoned, though Joffre telegraphed that the British were not to be given the impression that they were fighting alone. In Champagne, two French armies advanced on quite a wide front, but penetration of the first German line of defence proved deceptively easy. The second line of defence, which was beyond the range of French artillery, could not be breached and in the intervening space the French lost thousands of men. Fighting effectively ceased by mid-October. The French too had advanced about two miles. Overall, on all fronts, Allied casualties were heavier than German. Over the whole year, the French sustained about twice as many casualties as the Germans and five times as many as the British, but the military map was very little different from what it had been in January.

It was a different story in Eastern Europe. At the beginning of the year there had been much argument about the deployment of troops which was finally resolved by the Kaiser's decision that there should be a joint German–Austrian offensive. The personal rivalry between Falkenhayn and Hindenburg remained undimmed. There would be a German offensive in the north, through East Prussia which, it was hoped, would encircle the Russian armies. There would be an Austro-Hungarian offensive (with German support) in the Carpathians. In the north, after a series of feints, the German Tenth Army struck the Russians a series of severe blows in appalling weather conditions. They were frequently encircled and forced to surrender on a considerable scale. But there was a good deal of hit and miss about these manœuvres and the Russians also captured thousands of Germans. By the end of February it was apparent that the Russians would not be encircled and the general strategic position had not substantially altered. The Germans could not drive further east without risking their southern flank and the Russians could not chance the invasion of East Prussia when German internal lines of communication were so superior.

It was in conflict with the Austro-Hungarians that the Russians fancied their chances. Brusilov, commanding their Eighth Army, contemplated an offensive into Galicia. For his part, Conrad was anxious to relieve the fortress of Przemyśl. Its commander had assured him that the garrison would be starved out by mid-March. Sporadic fighting took place in atrocious conditions. In circumstances where thousands froze to death, the only consolation was that the cold prevented the gas shells from igniting. Men melted away from their units more effectively than did the ice. In mid-March Przemyśl fell to the Russians and for a fleeting few weeks Brusilov harried the Habsburg armies. In reality, the cold, the bewilderment, and shortages of food and ammunition meant that there was little to choose between the combat effectiveness of the two sides. Perception of this numbed parity gave the Germans their opportunity. Despite the Franco-British assaults in the West, troops were moved to the East though, as usual, there was disagreement about how they should be best employed. Hindenburg talked of sweeping down behind Warsaw from East Prussia. Falkenhayn initially talked about an attack on Serbia. They eventually agreed to Conrad's scheme for an attack east of Cracow from the Carpathian foothills. Conrad was nominally in command but the German commander of the newly formed German Eleventh Army, von Mackensen, had to have his orders directly approved by Falkenhayn. Protocol and pride were as complicated and tender in the East as they were in the West.

After preliminary bombardment, the German infantry broke through at Gorlice-Tarnow where attacks had been launched on 2 May on a front of more than twenty-five miles. The Russian Third Army, somewhat isolated and lacking reserves, pulled back. The Russians were now paying the price for quarrels amongst their commanders and a lack of co-ordination. The other Austro-German armies advanced and the opposing Russian armies retreated under pressure, but not in total disorder. Przemyśl, for example, was emptied of its supplies before being abandoned on 3 June. Was it wise to halt the Austro-German advance at the San river? Falkenhayn thought so, but Hindenburg advocated an attack in the north. Conrad was bothered by the Italians. It was the Kaiser who thought that Mackensen should keep up the momentum in Galicia. Lvov (Lemberg) fell on 22 June and he moved northwards in the direction of Brest-Litovsk. With Galicia and large areas of southern Poland in their hands, the German commanders met at Posen on 1 July to assess their next move. A massive encirclement from the north still attracted Hindenburg but frightened Falkenhayn. While it might virtually destroy the Russian armies, it could overextend Germany, lead to requests for more troops to be moved from the West and thus threaten that front. In the event, it was decided to attack across the Narev rather than the Niemen. The new German assaults began on 13 July and met with steady successes. In the south, Mackensen entered Lublin on 30 July and set off north-east towards Brest-Litovsk. Seeing what was coming, Grand Duke Nicholas abandoned Warsaw on 5 August and retreated east in fair order. By the end of the month, Brest-Litovsk fell, but at this point the momentum of advance faltered. In the north, Grodno and Vilna both fell to the Germans, but Hindenburg had reluctantly to acquiesce in the withdrawal of German troops to France and the Danube. Falkenhayn would not permit a winter campaign – it was already proving difficult to supply the large German armies that had travelled so far in the summer and autumn. He was satisfied that a great German success had been achieved. If the Allies had advanced two or three miles, the Germans had advanced two or three hundred miles.

Detecting that something was wrong, the tsar replaced his uncle as commander of the Russian armies on 5 September, but clearly more was needed than even his own hitherto unrevealed strategic gifts could supply. Explanations of the Russian retreat were abundant. It was sometimes suggested that German superiority in guns and shells made them invincible once (as happened by May) conditions and communications enabled it to be effectively deployed. Recent historical studies lay less stress upon this superiority and draw attention instead to the shortcomings of the Russian commanders. Given a more flexible handling of reserves, there was no inherent reason why the German breakthrough in May could not have been sealed off in the same manner as the Germans sealed off the Allied breakthroughs in the West. Yet, once the advance was under way there was not the organizational capacity to stop it – in the short term. The Russians lost around two million men in 1915 – although a half were prisoners of war. Commanders inevitably suffered a loss of confidence and morale among men slumped. Even so, in September, the Russians were capable of defeating some Austro-Hungarian forces and the Germans retained a higher opinion of the former than the latter. Above all, Russia was still in the war, bloody and bowed, but not eliminated. There was a 600-mile-long line between Riga on the Baltic and Czernowitz on the Romanian border and behind that line still stretched a lot of Russia. It was true that the Franco-British failure at Gallipoli might lead to fresh operations in the Caucasus but, the Turkish threat apart, Russia did not have to fight on two fronts. Despite their success, the Germans had the problems of administering Poland. It was thus possible that Russia could survive and fight on – if the matter was considered exclusively from a military standpoint. It was such a hope that was entertained in London and Paris, though it was recognized that effective co-ordination with St Petersburg would be little more feasible than it had been in 1915.

1916

By December 1915 it occurred to Joffre that, since there were now four Great Powers fighting against the Central Powers, a conference of their military representatives might not be out of place. He summoned them to his headquarters at Chantilly. The generals came to the unsurprising conclusion that Germany could be defeated if she were subjected to simultaneous offensives on the Western, Eastern and Italian fronts. There was a good deal of loose talk about co-ordination. Joffre had no doubt that the Western front should be the centre of activity and, as things stood, it appeared that a major

Russian or Italian contribution could be discounted. He had his eyes on the river Somme, more or less, so it happened, where the British and French lines joined. That would make a joint Franco-British operation inevitable. He had a private meeting with Haig (who had just replaced French as commander-in-chief of the British forces in France) on 29 December. Until his elevation, Haig had been showing some signs of doubt about an offensive, but he now allowed himself to be persuaded of its merits. He did not press his preference for Flanders. It was true that German defences in the chosen area were particularly strong, that it would be easy for German forces to withdraw without making any substantial communications or industrial sacrifice, but such appraisals did not deter. The British army was steadily expanding and, given some months in which to benefit from training, it could be a major force by the summer. Those who denied that a breakthrough was possible seemed to forget what the Germans had achieved in the East. So fortified, the Allies went about their preparations. In the wake of Gallipoli, the French felt confident that even the British had come to accept the primacy of the Western front.

Falkenhayn was also planning in December 1915. He identified Britain as Germany's principal opponent but recognized that, as yet, the German army could not cross the Channel. Unrestricted submarine warfare might perhaps sap British resources? In the meantime, it was vital to defeat France or persuade her to sue for peace. Britain would not fight on alone. It was therefore necessary to stake out a killing ground, a target which the French would feel compelled to defend but which would cost them dear. He settled on the fortress of Verdun, above the Meuse; its capture would be useful, but it was the symbol that mattered. Ironically, the French army was in the process of reorganizing Verdun's defences. Tidy minds determined that outlying forts were to be evacuated before a new system was implemented. Meanwhile, the Germans mobilized a massive quantity of artillery and attendant shells. Although Verdun's defenders became concerned, it was not until late January that the French High Command began to suspect that Verdun might be the target. Some inadequate precautions were taken. In the event, however, attackers outnumbered defenders by some five to two – not that soldiers were initially engaged in direct fighting.

On 21 February, the ferocious bombardment began, with about one million shells being fired on that day alone. Late in the afternoon, the infantry did move out and occupied the French front-line trenches, but they found to their cost that the bombardment had not in fact obliterated all opposition. Fort Douaumont fell to the Germans on 25 February. It was an ominous moment for General Pétain, who had been given command of the defence on the previous day. Joffre was in a quandary. He thought that one lesson of the war so far was that the fortress was an anachronism – that was why Douaumont had been stripped of its important guns. Besides, to send major reinforcements would jeopardize the Somme offensive. Nevertheless he was quickly made aware that, politically, surrender would not be acceptable. If Verdun fell, French morale would crumble – precisely the kind of calculation Falkenhayn hoped the French would make. However, he had his problems too. The scale of shell consumption enforced a lull in early March and Pétain seized his chance to reorganize, particularly to try to ensure that the vital single supply road was kept open. Additional troops and supplies did arrive. Pétain insisted on a rotation of troops, for the slaughter would otherwise have been unendurable. This policy worked, but it also meant that as the months passed a considerable portion of the French army had 'done time' at Verdun. The great German attacks of March and April were held and it began to seem that the Germans would indeed not pass. Consternation grew on the German side. Crown Prince Wilhelm was being deprived of the victory that he expected – though, as a commander, he kept his head rather better than did Falkenhayn. The chief of the German general staff neglected royal advice to rely on artillery and fed in German infantry in a struggle which had originally been designed to bleed the French white. Having husbanded his men and resources, Pétain was replaced at this juncture by Nivelle and Mangin who could be relied upon to be not so cautious, though there was not much else they could be relied upon for. Phosgene gas brought fresh horrors and the opposing soldiers began to suspect that there would be no end to this encounter. It is, indeed, difficult to say precisely when the battle for Verdun ended. German casualties exceeded French for the first time in August and, at the end of the month, Falkenhayn was relieved of his post and replaced by Hindenburg, with Ludendorff as his deputy. As if to emphasize Falkenhayn's responsibility for failure, the new leadership declined to press any further attacks. The French counter-attacked but it was not until mid-December that they regained the front line as it had existed in mid-February.

The human cost of Verdun cannot be precisely stated, and estimates vary, but the French losses – dead, wounded and missing – may have been nearly half a million and the German about 100,000 less. Whatever the exact figures, Verdun had an enormous psychological impact on the French nation. France had come through, but the scars were very evident in mind and body. The spectre of defeat had been avoided but the spectre of despair was near. Mutiny was in the air. To have been at Verdun marked a man for life. It was a drama, too, which remained defiantly French – a national experience which others could not quite understand or share in. One junior British officer, Captain Bernard Montgomery, took the comfortable view at the time that the French were not in the least anxious about Verdun. It was all part of 'our policy' to let the Germans beat themselves to death against a stone wall. He later recorded that his views on the fighting did not accord with the facts. With the exception of a small number of colonial troops, only French soldiers had been involved. Every belligerent nation had at least one such experience – for France it was Verdun.

Yet this grief was not quite as private as the French believed. Verdun was, in the last resort, simply a fortress (and a rather awkwardly placed one) in a particular segment of a single line. The intensity of the fighting there necessarily entailed an adjustment of the Allied plans as discussed at Chantilly in December. It meant that the anticipated offensive on the Somme became primarily a British responsibility. Haig did not intend to be hurried, despite Joffre's pleas that some relieving offensive was urgently needed. During the late spring, the size of the French contribution which would be committed dwindled with every passing month. Haig even toyed with postponing the attack until mid-August before agreeing to 1 July. He seemed confident in his preparations and did not seem perturbed by the fact that the Germans must have detected the impending 'Big Push'. Indeed, they looked down from their fortifications on a gentle ridge. British confidence rested in the anticipated effectiveness of the preliminary bombardment. It would range over a wide front rather than concentrate on specific strongpoints. Some three quarters of a million men were assembled – roughly seven British to one French – ready to clear a gap through which cavalry divisions would gallop to untold excitements in the interior. Rawlinson, commander of the Fourth Army, claimed that it was only a matter of walking over and occupying the desecrated trenches – but he may not have been serious. Most of the intending combatants were young volunteers who would have found it hard to tell whether or not he was joking.

They soon found out the truth. The British artillery began firing on 24 June, disposing of a million and a half shells before ceasing at 7.30 on 1 July. Thousands of men swarmed over the parapets and made for the German trenches. In no man's land, it soon became apparent that the heavy bombardment had not succeeded. The Germans, in many cases, had escaped relatively unscathed, since they were sheltering in 30-foot dug-outs in the chalk. The damage was, literally, only superficial. The small number of attackers who reached the barbed wire found even that intact and they had little opportunity for uninterrupted pruning. Successive lines of British soldiers were inexorably mown down. One corps did succeed in advancing for a mile, but that was very exceptional. By the evening, the stragglers crawled back to their starting place – if they were lucky. Nearly 60,000 casualties were sustained on this first day – and a third of them were killed. The French had delayed their assault until 9.30 and seem to have persuaded the Germans that they were not coming after all. They did advance in a consistent line, overrunning the German trenches and not sustaining such heavy casualties.

The battle could have been called off at once but Haig would not countenance such a course. Such lengthy preparations could not be written off because of one day, however tragic. But if the offensive was to continue there was certainly now no prospect of that cavalry dash through the German lines. Falkenhayn was equally insistent that the enemy should only advance over dead bodies. Joffre too urged the British on – it would be attrition but this time it would be the British who paid the price. The attacks therefore continued, on a battlefield churned up by shell craters and muddied over by rain. Through July and August the ghastly struggle continued and the casualties mounted on both sides. In September, Haig produced his secret weapon – the cumbersome and unreliable tank, whose movements as yet inspired more awe than fear amongst those Germans who observed it. Further attacks took place in September and October in deteriorating weather conditions, casualties at this stage being about equal on both sides. The British made small advances before the battle of the Somme can be said to have been ended by a snowstorm on 18 November. Exact figures are again impossible to provide, but over the four and a half months of the battle some three million men had been involved, of whom about a third were casualties. About half a million of these were German, over 400,000 British and under 200,000 French. The deepest Allied advance was eight miles. The battle of the Somme was the British equivalent of Verdun, with comparable emotional and psychological consequences. It was, indeed, arguably one extended encounter only made separate by the distortions of national perception. Certainly, it was the combined impact of the two struggles that brought about the replacement of Falkenhayn and, cumulatively, it was the losses sustained by the German army in the late summer of 1916 from both sources which sapped its strength and, ultimately, brought about its defeat. And its problems were not confined to the West.

In December 1915, at the Allied military conference, the Russian representatives painted a picture of an expanded Russian army ready for action in the late spring. There was talk of a descent on the Bulgarian coast, an assault which would counter the criticism that little had been done to assist Serbia. However, it went no further than talk. Instead, in the last days of the old year an attack was mounted in eastern Galicia against the Austro-Hungarians. The engagement was not a success. The Russians lost 50,000 men and achieved little in a fortnight's fighting. Failure stemmed not from shortcomings in equipment but from inadequate planning and preparation. Some of these lessons were slowly being learnt and the mood amongst the Russian generals was by no means pessimistic. After the German onslaught on Verdun, they were under pressure from Paris to launch a diversionary offensive. Taking advantage of numerical and material superiority (greater than that possessed by the Germans at Gorlice in May 1915), the Russians laid plans for an offensive east of Vilna. It opened on 18 March and has been described by Norman Stone as an episode 'that suggests commanders had lost such wits as they still possessed'. The engagement at Lake Narotch was a disaster – the Russians lost 100,000 men and the Germans only 20,000. In the longer term, too, it led the Russian generals in the north to suppose that they could not defeat the Germans.

The size and deployment of the Russian army was one of its major problems, but a consequence was that a generalization applicable to its performance in the north and west might not apply in the south. Despite the setback at Lake Narotch, the tsar convened a meeting in mid-April to discuss a June offensive. The northern commanders poured scorn on the idea of an attack north of the Pripet river, arguing that there was little chance of being able to break through the German lines. Brusilov, new commander of the South-Western Army group, was determined to lead an offensive of his own southwards and argued that such an expedition would make an attack in the Vilna region feasible. Partly in response to French pleas, he brought forward his starting date to 1 June. His plans were assisted by the fact that the Austrians had transferred some of their guns to the Italian front. In numerical terms, the opposing forces were roughly equal. Brusilov had brooded over the recent campaigns and concluded that speed and surprise were of the essence. The enemy should be prevented, by concealment and disguise, from guessing where precisely the major blow would fall. The intensity of his preparations was without parallel on the Russian front. He planned operations along a wide front and the reserves stood ready if a breakthrough was achieved. In numerical terms, the Russians had slightly the edge both in men and guns. The attack began on 4 June and, benefiting from surprise, made rapid progress, although Brusilov was disappointed by the abandonment of the assault which was to have been made by another Russian army to his right. The Russians speedily took many thousands of Habsburg troops prisoner, some of whom may have been suffering from Pan-Slav sentiment or, more prosaically, have proved unable to understand the language in which their commanders addressed them. Once again, although word of Brusilov's intentions had reached the Austrian commanders, there was neither the will nor the energy to take effective counter-steps. Thus, despite the prevailing confidence, catastrophe had arrived. In the course of a week it has been estimated that the Austro-Hungarian army lost over half its forces in the East. It was a shattering setback from which it could not recover; only German aid could restore some semblance of order.

It was a further blow to Falkenhayn to be compelled again to think about Austria-Hungary. A few divisions were withdrawn from the Western front and some from elsewhere were hurriedly rushed to the scene. The absence of activity on other sections of the Russian front made these rearrangements possible. Rail communications worked in favour of the Germans – and against the Russians. After his breakthrough, Brusilov was in a quandary. His success was greater than had been anticipated, but the manner of achieving it precluded further advance. He did not have large reserves, partly by his own design. Should he drive on in the south-west against the Austro-Hungarians or move north, enlist the effort of the neighbouring Russian army group under Evert, and attack the Germans? He decided on the latter course though, to his chagrin, he was to find that his colleague had no enthusiasm for attack. When he was persuaded to do so in early July, it was a failure. Other generals proved eager to let Brusilov have troops – for his own losses had not been insignificant – if that meant that the battle would once more take a south-westerly direction. Brusilov attacked again on 28 July. Two days later Hindenburg assumed control of the front from the Baltic down as far as Tarnopol, leaving the Austrian Archduke Karl to command only the remaining section to the Romanian border, and he had the German Seeckt on his staff to keep a watchful eye. Inexorably, at various military levels, the Austro-Hungarian army was ceasing to exist as an independent entity.

The consequence of this reorganization was that in August there was a more determined resistance to Brusilov, though he still made some progress, reaching the foothills of the Carpathians. Offensives against Kowel (in the centre of the front) were not successful, partly because the lessons which had brought Brusilov his original successes had not been absorbed elsewhere. In any case, there was simply not time for the careful preparations in advance that he had made in the past. Russian casualties mounted and by the end of September there was little to choose between the losses sustained by both sides over the four-month period. Brusilov had pushed back the line but he had not fundamentally altered the strategic situation. If the gains were encouraging, the price was heavy. Losses on such a scale could not but have reverberations elsewhere. On the other hand, it could be said that, despite the scepticism sometimes shown, Britain, France and Russia had, to a degree, beneficially timed their military operations and almost acted as an alliance.

It was the belief that the Allies were succeeding which helped to persuade Romania to declare war on Austria-Hungary at the end of August. Bucharest had long coveted Romanian-speaking areas of Transylvania in Hungary but when the Central Powers were in the ascendancy had refused to be drawn to the Allied side. The French, in particular, were predisposed to believe that the ill-led and illiterate Romanian army would tip the balance in favour of the Allies. So eager were the Romanians to show their mettle that they marched briskly into Transylvania, but they were stopped at the end of

September by an Austro-German force under Falkenhayn – who was also particularly anxious to show his mettle. In the south, a German–Bulgarian–Turkish force pushed steadily across the country and captured the Black Sea port of Constanza on 23 October. It was not taking long to discover that Romania could not be defended. Falkenhayn moved steadily from the north-west towards Bucharest and made contact with Mackensen outside the city on 27 November. After fierce fighting, the Germans entered the capital on 6 December. The Russians had sent in some troops as well as supplies but they too now retreated to the north-east of the country where the Romanians established a new capital at Jássy. There they could pretend to be independent and reflect on their folly. The Germans had no interest in fighting on. Their troops could be more profitably used elsewhere and there was just the chance that rump Romania could later be persuaded to change sides and seek territorial compensation at Russian expense. All that remained was for their allies, the Bulgarians and the Turks, to quarrel over their conquests.

The Romanians had hoped that they might receive substantial support from the impressive-sounding *Armées Alliées en Orient* established in Greece. The force was supposed to be commanded by the French General Sarrail, but not all the contributing governments seemed to take this view of his status. Inevitably, messages reached Salonika from Paris suggesting an expedition which would relieve the pressure on Verdun. Falkenhayn too seems to have thought that there was some connexion between the two theatres because he sent some German troops to Bulgaria. Serrail made a gesture in moving a little nearer the frontier – though not across it. It was unwise to go too far north because the allegedly pro-German Greek government might cause trouble. However, by August, his army stiffened by Albanian units, Serrail was on the brink of attacking the Bulgarians. So the Germans advised the Bulgarians to take the first step and they did indeed catch some Serb, Greek and French units unawares. The British distinguished themselves in blowing up bridges. In September, however, Serb forces retaliated, driving the Bulgarians back and on 19 November French and Serb cavalry captured the important town of Monastir. By this stage all the belligerents were running short of supplies and feeling the cold. Winning the war would have to wait for better weather.

The Italians had also promised their allies in December 1915 that they would make a contribution to the common effort in the summer of 1916, though there was nothing very specific about the offer. It was evidence, however, of Cadorna's conviction that Italy could not 'fight her own *piccola guerra*' divorced from the activities of her allies. By the same token, when messages from Paris also reached Rome in February 1916, the Italian commander responded by a short, not very sharp and certainly futile week's activity in early March. It was called the fifth battle of the Isonzo. By September 1917 there were to be six more unsuccessful battles of the same name. In December 1915, while Falkenhayn had been urging others that the best way of striking at Britain was to attack France, Conrad was urging upon him that the best way of striking at France was to attack Italy. The idea of such an assault was not novel; nor was Falkenhayn's negative response. Sensing that a thrust from the Trentino to the Italian plain would isolate the Isonzo and Alpine fronts, Conrad nevertheless decided to make preparations, showing an unfounded confidence in his north-eastern front. Launched in mid-May, the offensive made good progress and by the end of the month the Austrian forces had captured two towns, Arsiero and Asiago, which then opened the way to the plains. By this stage, Cadorna had marshalled his armies with some skill and over the next fortnight the Austrian advance petered out. The Italian commander launched a successful counter-attack, though the outcome of the campaign might have been different had it not been for Brusilov's Galician offensive. Men and guns were rushed away from Italy to this front, though to no avail. If Conrad could have concentrated his forces upon only one enemy he would have won, but that option was not open. Italian losses were nearly twice those of the Austrians, but that was not good enough. *Italia delenda est* – and that had not happened. Cadorna inevitably celebrated with another assault on the Isonzo in August, this time capturing Gorizia and Monte San Michele. 'Here was scientific war at last,' commented G. M. Trevelyan. He noted that the Italians had now progressed to sporting shrapnel helmets while their captives were still in slouchy, dishevelled forage caps. However, in September, October and November, when three further distinct battles were fought in the area, the Austrians had moved in considerable additional forces. Further Italian gains were slight and achieved at heavy cost. Nevertheless at the close of the year the Italians could be satisfied with their performance and war had even been confidently declared upon Germany on 24 August.

Translated from Russian commander-in-chief to viceroy of

Transcaucasia, Grand Duke Nicholas was anxious about the distribution of Turkish troops after their success at Gallipoli. Calculating that they would appear on the Russian frontier in March 1916, General Yudenich was ordered to take the offensive in January. The Turks were driven back to Erzerum and the town and its defenders surrendered in mid-February. Yudenich pushed on further south. A Black Sea expedition led to the capture of Trebizond. Troops from Gallipoli did arrive, but the Turkish counter-attacks could not be sustained. From mid-summer, Turkish Armenia was in Russian hands. On the other hand, the Turks could celebrate the British surrender at Kut in Mesopotamia on 29 April. In the preceding months, various attempts under several commanders had been made to relieve the beleaguered garrison but without success. Surrender was a humiliating experience which might well have an impact on Britain's standing in the Middle East and India. That political possibility, plus the treatment of the British captives, led to a desire for an expedition and by the end of the year it was ready to advance. On the other hand, at the tip of Arabia, Turkish forces seemed poised to attack Aden, though that was a position they remained in for the rest of the war. June 1916 saw a further complication in the peninsula. The Hashemite rulers of the Hejaz staged a revolt against their Turkish overlords and captured Mecca and Jeddah. But they failed to take Medina, where the main Turkish garrison was stationed. The railway was not cut and Turkish reinforcements began to arrive. It looked as though the revolt would peter out. One of the reasons why it did not was the arrival of T. E. Lawrence, who developed the remarkable guerrilla activity which could only occur to someone who lacked any formal military training. The Turks were forced to deploy an increasing number of troops simply to keep the line open. Further north, the British and the Turks were engaged in a series of battles in the Sinai peninsula. By December, British troops had reached the town of El Arish, only to find that the Turks had abandoned it. It was unlikely, however, that the Turks would be found toothless in Gaza.

T. E. Lawrence had a rival for ingenuity in German East Africa – von Lettow-Vorbeck. He had even had the temerity to invade Kenya. Aided by a convenient swarm of wild bees, his men in November 1915 had driven off an Indian force which had attempted to take the port of Tanga. Here was a challenge fit for that former hero of the veld, General Smuts, and those South African troops who had successfully taken German South West Africa in the summer of 1915. Belgian, Portuguese and Indian troops also joined in the chase, but the German general proved elusive. Having failed to bring this campaign to a successful conclusion, Smuts left for London at the end of the year to advise on how the British empire should win the world war.

That it could be won still did not seem impossible, though to put the answer in that form reveals how expectations had changed after two and a half years. As always happened at the end of a year there was a flurry of political speculation. Men wrote in their diaries what they would still not say in public. But if the war was to go on the identity of the victorious alliance was still unclear. On balance, it had been a successful year for the Allies, though that did not mean that victory was in sight. The Central Powers had not gained fresh ground but they might feel that they could soon take Russia out of the war. Then the picture might look very different.

1917

In January 1917, the disappointments of the previous year produced a mood of uncertainty. Talk of peace was in the air and President Wilson supposed that the belligerents might contemplate 'peace without victory'. Throughout Europe, politicians oscillated between taking such an aspiration seriously and planning the crucial breakthrough. New men with some new ideas – like Lloyd George – had just come to power, though even they had little notion of the dramatic changes which would occur in the coming months. As a new prime minister, Lloyd George appeared to believe that his vigour and energy would transform the management of the war effort. In France, there was a new commander-in-chief. Nivelle, successful organizer of the final counter-attacks at Verdun, replaced Joffre. In Germany, Ludendorff was in the ascendancy, but both he and Hindenburg urged that the land war could be won at sea. The argument in Berlin about unrestricted submarine warfare, which had been rumbling on for many months, now came to a head. To favour such a policy betrayed a certain pessimism about the military status quo. Since an acceptable compromise peace did not appear possible, the only alternative was to starve Britain – still considered the principal enemy. Opponents of this course drew attention to the dangers it entailed. There was particular anxiety about provoking the

United States into the war. Ludendorff replied that even if this did happen, the consequences would not be dramatic, in the short term. The United States was, in practice, already assisting the Allies and, besides, it would take time for the American army to become an effective fighting force – and the U-boats might prevent the troops from reaching Europe. German military confidence in naval prowess was touchingly complete and, after intense discussion, the fateful decision to begin unrestricted submarine warfare was taken on 1 February.

For their part, the Allies again conferred. It was once more asserted, this time at a gathering in Rome in January that, by acting independently, they were failing to make the best use of their collective resources. Lloyd George took advantage of the meeting-place to suggest that they might show a new spirit of co-operation by concentrating on the Italian front. That proposal alarmed the Italians as much as it did the French and British military. Great co-operation was displayed among them in defeating it. Even so, the delegates agreed that the Allies would seek to mount spring offensives in concert.

The new French commander had a plan which he was particularly anxious to sell to the British. Having broken through at Verdun, it seemed that there was no reason why he could not do the same again, if he had larger forces at his disposal. There was some talk of novelty, but it reality there was little more in his plans than a fresh emphasis upon speed and size, coupled with the extended use of the rolling artillery barrage which he had employed at Verdun. Nivelle set great store by psychological preparation. His subordinates, right down to company commanders, were given specific times for the achievement of particular targets. If they were stressed frequently enough they might even be reached. He wanted nothing less than an all-out offensive aimed at overwhelming the main German forces. French troops were to strike the Noyon salient from the south, along the Aisne river. The British were to play their part by mounting a major diversion around Arras a few days before. Confident in his command of English, Nivelle even came to London in person to persuade the prime minister to endorse his plans. Lloyd George attached much importance to heads and faces and Nivelle's features were engagingly similar to his own. He gave his support. At the Franco-British conference held in Calais on 26 February he revealed his willingness to subordinate Haig to Nivelle for the duration of the offensive –

indeed, had not Haig and Robertson (chief of the imperial general staff) objected so strongly, he would have gone further. The prime minister seemed more likely to be predestined for success under a French than a Scottish Calvinist. Nivelle himself did not spend time worrying about whether his forces would head for the North Sea, Brussels, the Meuse or the Rhine once they had broken through. At that stage, they would be able to do as they pleased.

Ludendorff decided not to attack in the West in early 1917 – a magnanimous response to the fact that his forces were very considerably outnumbered by the Allies. Indeed, the German commanders took realism about their numerical position a stage further. Even before it became apparent that Nivelle was preparing a surprise in the Noyon salient they decided to retreat in that area and establish themselves behind what the Allies flatteringly called the Hindenburg line. The result of withdrawing some twenty miles to the east – the operation was carried out from late February to early April – was to establish a much shorter line requiring fewer divisions to hold it. Not only this, but a complex pattern of defence in depth was constructed and reserve troops, prepared for a counter-offensive, were kept further back than was customarily the case. The land in front of the line was laid to waste so that no shelter, man-made or natural, remained. It was no longer, if it had ever been, promising territory in which to attack.

These activities had not gone unremarked by the Allies. There was even some satisfaction that the Germans had yielded ground without a fight. However, alarm on the Allied side now began to spread. Haig seemed to have more solid grounds for unease than merely dissatisfaction with his own subordination. French generals grumbled, particularly those who had been passed over in favour of Nivelle. In mid-March, too, the French government fell and the new minister of war, Painlevé, was known to have been against Nivelle's appointment and suspicious of the plan. In favour of Painlevé was the fact that he could count. In favour of caution was the fact that the new prime minister, Ribot, was a mere eighty years old. Not wishing to jeopardize a promising career, he summoned a meeting of ministers and generals which took place on 6 April in the presidential railway carriage at Compiègne station (Nivelle was installed in the chateau). Critics were most vocal and Nivelle was reduced to arguing that the morale of his troops had risen sharply and would slump if the action were abandoned. There was one other factor in his favour. On

12 March revolution broke out in Petrograd and the tsar abdicated three days later. The Provisional government in Russia was committed to continuing the war but might not be able to do so since its own position was precarious. It was impossible to predict what would happen in the East and unless a blow was struck at this point in the West it might not ever be possible on such numerically favourable terms. Dramatically, Nivelle offered his resignation and received instead a vote of confidence. The offensive was to go ahead. On the same day, for reasons subsequently to be discussed, the United States declared war on Germany. Nivelle had to show what could be done before the new Associate (not Ally) attempted to bring its influence to bear. The temporary inhabitants of the presidential coach did not wish to see the fulcrum of the world rest anywhere other than Compiègne railway station.

Meanwhile, the British had already begun a massive bombardment around Arras, prior to their diversionary attack. Haig pronounced his men 'confident and seasoned' but could scarcely see them in the driving snow which coincided with the eventual day of the attack – 9 April. Good progress was made on the first day, particularly the capture of the major part of Vimy ridge by the Canadians, but over the next few days it could not be sustained. Haig paused to regroup and wait for Nivelle. The French had indeed gathered together four formidable armies, numbering some 1,200,000 men, roughly double the total of their opponents. On the other hand, the notion of surprise had by this time virtually disappeared and the Germans were established in superior natural positions, which they had strongly fortified. After preliminary bombardment, Nivelle launched the assault early on 16 April. It soon became apparent that many of the German positions had not been put out of action but, in awful conditions, the attack was pressed forward along a forty-mile front. Although some ground was gained in places, it was at heavy cost and even by the end of the first day it was apparent that it would not succeed. Undaunted, Nivelle urged his commanders on, although French dead mounted to 40,000 after the first few days. Naturally, news of the disaster soon reached Paris and there were moves to replace Nivelle. Even so, the fighting continued and on 5 May the French could claim to have cleared the Chemin des Dames ridge. Thereafter, however, the fighting petered out. The French may have sustained around 150,000 casualties, the Germans rather less. Having dismissed Mangin, commander of the Sixth

Army, Nivelle was himself replaced on 15 May by Pétain. Failure had deeper consequences than the replacement of one general by another. Over the next six weeks the French army was in a precarious position. It is normally suggested that many units mutinied, though Pétain himself refused to use the word. By the late summer, order was virtually restored, but even so Pétain was not anxious to expose his forces to another major engagement. It was the British turn to take the offensive.

Haig had long believed that it would be sensible to attack in Flanders where the flat land deprived the Germans of the defensive positions they had used to such good effect. Success in this region would compel the Germans to pull back from Belgium and northern France. Although the full extent of the crisis in the French army was concealed from the British, it was obvious that it had suffered severely. Unless the British moved swiftly, the Germans could redeploy the units they had transferred to the Aisne. It was also important to try to prevent them moving to the Eastern front where the situation from the Allied standpoint was deteriorating rapidly. Haig's wish to mount an offensive received support from the admiralty, which was anxious to eliminate the destructive German U-boat bases on the Belgian North Sea coast. He claimed that success would be reasonably certain and even if a triumph was not obtained the enemy would be worn down. Haig's optimism was not dented by information about the condition of the French army relayed by Pétain himself – who was not enthusiastic about the British plans. He was not deterred by Lloyd George's sudden enthusiasm for the Italian front. And his confidence seemed justified by the brilliant success of 7 June when the important Messines ridge was captured – with the aid of about a million tons of TNT. It was a triumph in particular for the cautious Plumer who had been driving shafts under the German lines for months. It was this victory, coupled with alarm about the level of shipping losses and the consequential ability to wage war into 1918, which persuaded the government to give Haig his chance.

Haig did not rush. Indeed, it was not until 31 July that the first attack in what was to be known as the third battle of Ypres was launched. Haig had envisaged an interval between the Messines operation and the main assault but it had been delayed unduly by continuing political hesitations and his decision to give the main role in the Flanders campaign to the Fifth Army under Gough. Plumer's feats in carrying out a battle according to plan and losing less men than the enemy in the process seemed to brand him as unsuitable for the adventure that was about to begin. Gough attacked and immediately ran into difficulties, but it was pointed out that the casualties were appreciably lower than those sustained on the first day of the Somme and more progress was made. But the fortnight's heavy bombardment which had preceded the 'surprise' attack had devastated the delicate network of drains and dikes which prevented the area from becoming a swamp. Meteorological reports had disclosed that heavy rain was a feature of August weather – and it turned out that the rainfall level was well above average. In such conditions, Gough made two further attacks in mid-August, after which he reported to Haig that tactical success was unlikely or could only be achieved at too heavy a price. Haig responded by giving the major role instead to Plumer. Eschewing a dramatic breakthrough, Plumer again organized a series of set-piece battles in late September and was aided by better weather. The third attack, in early October, afforded a passage on to part of Passchendaele ridge. Both Plumer and Gough now felt that the offensive should be halted. The Belgian ports could not be reached before winter and the idea of an amphibious operation in support had already been called off.

Haig knew the feelings of his commanders, but reasoned that control of the entire Passchendaele ridge would give him a more easily defended line for the winter. So ensued a further month's campaign from early October to early November. The weather conditions once more deteriorated and gave this final stretch of the campaign its evil reputation. The capture by the Canadians of Passchendaele village on 6 November still did not give complete control of the ridge, but even Haig was now persuaded to call a halt. British casualties since the campaign began exceeded 300,000 while German losses over the entire Western front were about 275,000. Moreover, although the British had advanced, the Germans were not demoralized and had not disappeared. In wearing down the Germans it looked as though the British would be exhausted first. Haig's defence of the attrition in Flanders was that he gave the French army the quiet time it needed. He could observe that the French had even managed a successful little sortie from Verdun. However, it does not seem that the Germans intended to attack the French and Haig's solicitude was unnecessary. It seems unlikely that Pétain actually requested him to continue his attacks for the sake of the French army.

German commanders subsequently claimed that the strength of their Fourth Army had been sapped during this campaign – but not to a significantly greater extent than the British themselves.

Despite the criticism and his own disappointment, Haig had not yet finished. Reasoning that the Germans would have supposed that he had, he looked around for a modest operation which would restore British prestige and, as he put it, 'strike a theatrical blow against Germany before the winter'. The dramatic element in the ensuing assault on the Hindenburg Line, across the St Quentin Canal and on to Cambrai (considerably further south and away from the mud), launched on 25 November, was provided by massed tanks. This time the plan worked and, on a six-mile front, tanks and infantry advanced further in four hours than had been achieved in four months. Yet the speed of advance brought its own problems. The supporting artillery was too far in the rear and the Germans regrouped, bombarded and counter-attacked. The British were pushed back more or less to the point from which they had started. However, at the beginning of December, some took comfort from the performance of the tanks and others observed what benefits might follow from a surprise attack that really was a surprise.

By any standards, however, 1917 was a disappointing year for Britain and France on the Western front. Elsewhere, however, it threatened to prove disastrous. In the spring, as they had promised, the Italians again mounted an attack on the Isonzo front. By the time fighting had ceased in early June, the Austrians had regained ground they had initially lost. Cadorna switched at once to an attack in the mountains of the Trentino. However, two and a half weeks at high altitudes proved sufficient even for crack Italian Alpine troops – for summer spectacle, there was nothing in the war to compare with this engagement. Under Allied pressure, Cadorna knew that it was time to go back to the Isonzo front. He assembled a major force, but in a month's fighting, from mid-August to mid-September, the Italians failed to do more than make incidental gains at considerable cost. Vital defensive points still remained in Austrian hands. Even so, the Austrian commanders concluded that a further Italian assault might be successful and suggested that it might be forestalled by an offensive. German troops, some from Russia and some from the Western front, were to strengthen the Austrian forces in a concerted attempt to defeat, or at least significantly weaken, Italy. In late September Cadorna decided not to renew the offensive. By the middle of October it was apparent that the enemy was increasing his strength on the Isonzo front but there was considerable disagreement among the Italian commanders about where the attack would come and how it would be best countered.

The bombardment opened early on 24 October. It was brief but of an intensity not hitherto experienced on this front. The Italian Second Army reeled back before a German attack in the area near Caporetto. Other Austrian and German units pushed ahead in different sectors – from Trentino to the coast. Cadorna accepted the need to retreat but was not expeditious in carrying it out. Capello, commander of the Second Army, had been in a high fever before the battle began and nothing that had since happened had improved his health. The initial plan had been to hold the line of the Tagliamento river but by early November that proved impossible, so rapid and comprehensive was the advance. There was a widespread impression, shared to the full by many Italian soldiers, that the Italian army had collapsed. Civilians and soldiers fled in disarray and it was often difficult to distinguish the two categories. Many prisoners were taken and the effective fighting strength of the Italian army was halved. Nevertheless, the rout was not complete. The remaining divisions, though sadly short of equipment, regrouped in relatively good order behind the river Piave. General Cadorna was replaced as commander-in-chief by General Diaz in mid-November. By this time, too, a total of eleven British and French divisions had been rushed to Italy (the British were commanded by Plumer) to form a reserve behind the Italian line and assist in restoring confidence. The position was still precarious, but the superior Austro-German forces had advanced so quickly that they ran short of supplies. In the remaining weeks of the year they made several attempts to cross the Piave, but did not succeed.

The disaster of Caporetto, it was said, convinced the Allied leaders that they needed to co-ordinate their policies more closely. On 5 November, Lloyd George, Painlevé and Orlando, the respective prime ministers, met at Rapallo and produced an agreement to set up a supreme war council on which there would be political and military representation. It would meet regularly at Versailles and, no doubt, exercise a watching brief over the conduct of the war. At least it gave General Cadorna a new job.

Not present at Rapallo was a representative of the Russian government. Within hours of the meeting, Lenin seized power in

Petrograd. Hostilities on the Eastern front ceased in mid-December when an armistice was concluded. Negotiations for a peace treaty then opened between the Bolsheviks and the Central Powers. Russia was effectively out of the war. In the summer, Kerensky had still allowed himself to be persuaded that a further offensive was possible. In the months following the overthrow of the tsar the Germans had not attacked, calculating that inaction on their part might turn the situation inside Russia to their advantage. They merely facilitated the return to Russia from Switzerland of Lenin and other Bolsheviks. In a deteriorating situation, Kerensky hoped that a successful offensive in Galicia would restore discipline in the army. Brusilov had been made commander-in-chief in June and he prepared three armies to capture Lvov. In late June and early July the attack was launched and gained some success against both the Austrians and Germans. But the advance was only temporary. Success had been due to surprise and the Austro-Germans rallied and then went on to the offensive themselves. Brusilov had the melancholy experience of seeing all the territory he had won so dramatically in 1916 pass into enemy hands. It was the last Russian offensive, though the Germans were still cautious. They had no wish to enter Petrograd but consolidated their position on the Baltic by capturing Riga in early September. It was now all over bar the peace treaty, though that was to take longer to conclude than they had anticipated.

The British could draw comfort only from their success in the Middle East. General Allenby, warned by the astute Lloyd George to avoid a four-legged entry, walked rather self-consciously into Jerusalem on 11 December. The city had surrendered a few days earlier. Here was a glorious spectacle after a series of rather dispiriting battles against the Turks around Gaza in previous months. Masterminding Turkish resistance in the last of these encounters was no less a figure than Falkenhayn. However, his attempt to recapture Jerusalem just after Christmas proved a failure. In Mesopotamia, Baghdad had been taken in mid-March by General Maude. The Turks retreated, weary but in good order, a further fifty miles and awaited a renewed British advance. Ramadi, on the Euphrates, was captured at the end of September, though cholera took General Maude in mid-November. Control of Jerusalem and Baghdad naturally raised British standing in the Arab world, as did the intermittent assistance given to Feisal and his Arab forces. Even so, Ottoman Turkey was not defeated. Indeed, the Russian revolution eased its problems on that frontier, except that Armenian soldiers continued to find considerable satisfaction in fighting the Turks. The Turks found equal satisfaction in killing Armenians.

No one could pretend that the world war would be settled in the Middle East, but for the British at least their success opened up a number of interesting possibilities. It helped to take their minds off other problems. Although they did not take their minds off the Levant, the French had to content themselves with the scarcely less exotic internal history of Greece. General Sarrail, who controlled Salonika, found Paris and London unwilling to furnish him with more troops and the front remained quiet. He did try one attack in May 1917, but that fizzled out in a fortnight because of the non-cooperation of the Serbs for whose benefit it was launched. At long last it proved possible, with the assistance of Venizelos, to force the king of Greece to leave his country. A French ship obligingly sailed him to Germany, the country of his ancestors. His second son proved more amenable to the Allied cause and Venizelos bravely declared war on Germany and Bulgaria in July. Sustained bickering between British and French officers successfully kept military action to a minimum, though it was frequently thought to be a real possibility. Sarrail was replaced by a more energetic French general in December and there were local fears that the troops might see action in the coming year. It was disappointing to have to report that in German East Africa, von Lettow-Vorbeck was still roaming around at will, inflicting heavy casualties upon the British when he encountered them. It was then his custom to disappear with captured supplies. Even specially drafted Nigerian troops could not uncover his tracks. It was the least of Britain's military problems, but galling none the less.

1918

At previous turning points, the war had resolutely refused to turn, but at the beginning of 1918 there did seem grounds for believing that it would prove the decisive, if not the concluding, year. The pressure seemed to be on the Allies. The Austro-Germans steadily consolidated their grasp over vast areas of Eastern Europe. The Russian empire was in process of dissolution as the Baltic peoples exchanged masters and the Ukraine prepared for a sort of independence under German auspices. Each week that passed saw the transfer of German divisions from the Eastern to the Western front. Russia was out of the war and it seemed that Italy was only precariously in it. Neither the British nor the French were in a position to mount offensives. Ludendorff believed that the time had come for Germany to launch a major attack in the West for the first time since 1914. Planning for Operation 'Michael' began in mid-November 1917 with a target of the late spring for the decisive offensive. Ground conditions would then be favourable and it would be possible to achieve victory before the American presence was felt. It was calculated that, for a time, Germany would have a numerical superiority over the Allies in the West and this novel fact would tip the balance.

The Americans were very much in the minds of the opposing European leaders. Although they had been in the war for some nine months, their military impact was minimal. The build-up of American divisions in the last months of 1917 had been slow, reaching a total of some 175,000 at the opening of the year. While they looked remarkably healthy and confident to European eyes, there was the knowledge that this confidence was based on inexperience. Pershing, commander-in-chief of the American Expeditionary Force was determined to establish a self-contained United States Army and not allow his men to be swallowed by the military appetites of the Europeans. The problems of constructing a major army were considerable and it was vital for the Germans that they were not overcome before their offensive struck home. After Caporetto, the target for the size of the American army was raised substantially, but at the beginning of the year it was still only a paper force.

Ludendorff decided to strike the British on the old battleground of the Somme, with the main effort being made where the British and French sectors joined. The possibility of attacking the French to the south was considered, but rejected. They had too much space into which to retreat. The initial preferences were gradually elaborated and at a conference on 21 January Ludendorff came to firm conclusions. The main thrust would be between Arras and St Quentin. If the attack was successful, the British would retreat to the north-west to secure their communications to the Channel ports and the French would retreat to the south-west in order to protect Paris. German armies would exploit this gap and encircle the British on their open right flank. Ludendorff also placed stress upon the tactics to be employed. He had ceased to believe in the efficacy of the massive initial bombardment. Experience at Riga and Caporetto suggested that an intense whirlwind barrage was the answer. Relying upon small and well-equipped infantry groups, the attackers would move across the field of battle with great speed.

It was apparent by early February that an attack was likely and the intelligence assessments proved fairly accurate. Yet, despite the creation of the Allied supreme war council there was little agreement on the appropriate reaction. After Passchendaele, Lloyd George had been reluctant to increase British force levels in Flanders for fear that Haig would again be tempted to attack. He also claimed that a German assault on the Western front would be no more successful in bringing the war to an end than had been previous Allied efforts. He looked again at south-eastern Europe and the Middle East. Aware that he now had responsibility for forty additional miles of the front, Haig pressed for half a million more men. He did manage to reach an arrangement with Pétain to switch reserves if circumstances demanded it. It had the unfortunate effect of justifying the relative weakness of the most southerly of the British armies, that commanded by Gough, where the attack was in fact to fall most effectively.

The massive but swift bombardment began early on 21 March over a sixty-mile line. The Germans pushed Gough's army back nearly forty miles by the end of the fifth day and threatened Amiens. The position in the north was better initially but soon came under intense pressure. In the French sector, which was also now under attack, the Germans took Noyon. Pétain and Haig met late at night on 24 March to assess the position. Confronted by the collapse of the Fifth Army, which threatened to become a complete rout, Haig appealed for the reserves he had been promised. Pétain still feared that the main German attack had not yet come and reserves would have to be moved to cover Paris. Haig supposed that the Frenchman was willing to leave the British to their inevitable fate while he prepared, probably unavailingly, to defend Paris. He appealed to London stating that in this desperate situation a supreme commander had to be appointed. A high-level meeting was arranged at Doullens on 26 March attended by Milner and Wilson (the new war secretary and chief of the imperial general staff respectively). Clemenceau, who had been prime minister since mid-November, remained a tiger in defeat. Haig and Pétain confronted each other. In an emotional session, Foch became the hero of the hour, showing a willingness to fight in front of, in and behind Amiens. He was appointed 'co-ordinator' of the Allied armies on the Western front, a post significantly short of commander-in-chief, a title still unacceptable to the British cabinet, though not now to Haig. What was most important, however, was that reinforcements were shifted from the French front to help the British. In fact, the German momentum was already faltering and, in early April, despite another assault, Amiens did not fall. Ludendorff ended the attack. It seemed to have been successful since his armies had penetrated some forty miles on a front of the same length. They had captured many prisoners and guns and caused around 150,000 casualties, chiefly among the British. Their own losses were heavy but probably lower than that total. It was a successful but not decisive attack. The British army was still in the field and the British and French forces had not been separated and the vital wedge driven between them. It was not even the case that the territory gained was worthwhile – Ludendorff himself had abandoned large parts of it when he retreated behind the Hindenburg line. He now again had longer lines of entrenchments to defend, and he did not have the men. Indeed, arguably, it was insufficient numerical superiority which prevented him from sustaining his advance and permitted the Allies to regroup and save themselves. And, as time passed, the spectre of the Americans increased. Their role in March was only marginal, but it was significant none the less. Pershing, at least temporarily, was prepared to let American troops serve under foreign command. Protocol was also dispensed with in certain other respects.

Ludendorff did not delay long before making his next move. Still not abandoning hope of victory, he shifted his next attack to Flanders, on both sides of the Lys river, against the British and the Portuguese. The German commanders had considerably fewer troops at their disposal and the front on which they attacked was much shorter, but nevertheless the initial assault was again successful. Haig rushed what reinforcements he could find to the scene of the breakthrough and begged Foch for some French divisions, initially without much success. There was talk of evacuating Calais, even of flooding the countryside. British troops fought tenaciously and the German impetus faded, failing to capture either Hazebrouck or Ypres. Even so, the attacks continued spasmodically, culminating in fierce battles around Mont Kemmel in late April. His successes cost him dear and he was no nearer the decisive break-through which he sought. However, it still seemed tantalizingly close and he knew that the British had been badly mauled.

His third offensive was prepared in great secrecy. The area selected was the Chemin des Dames, the highway along the Aisne river, the scene of bitter struggles in the past. The French remained convinced that the attack would probably come at the junction of the British and French lines. After a massive artillery bombardment, German shock troops broke through on the morning of 27 May. They crossed the Aisne River and three days later they had reached the Marne near Château-Thierry – a drive of about thirty miles and only some forty miles from Paris. There were signs of panic in the capital. Ludendorff's problem was that this attack had originally been designed to draw away reserves from the north prior to what he hoped would be a decisive thrust in Flanders. It now seemed so successful that it appeared madness to stop it. In this desperate position, Pershing again agreed to waive his insistence that American troops should only fight as an independent army. Units of the American Third Division joined French troops in throwing the Germans back in their repeated efforts to cross the Marne. Another American division had been successful a few days earlier in capturing the village of Cantigny in its first offensive of the war. And the US Second Division successfully blocked a determined German drive in early June west of Château-Thierry on the way to Paris. Over 275,000 American troops crossed the Atlantic in June, the highest monthly figure yet achieved, and after their performance in these battles their fighting quality could not be dismissed. The arrival of fresh troops was some compensation for the heavy Allied losses; the Germans had no such relief. Ludendorff, however, discounted the combat-readiness of most of these new arrivals and still believed that he held the initiative – but he could not delay for long. The salient he had established was vulnerable, but to withdraw would damage the momentum of progress. Equally, if it was to be adequately defended, he would not be in a position to take away troops for the Flanders campaign. He decided to launch two more modest attacks beginning on 9 June but, partly because the French had advance information, this offensive ran into difficulties at an early stage. General Mangin's defence in depth was well-planned and a vigorous counter-attack, with American participation, led Ludendorff to abandon the operation in the middle of the month. German losses had been considerable and the numerical balance shifted against him. This final drive could not even be regarded as a tactical success.

Even so, Ludendorff had not given up. He still contemplated a final drive against the British in Flanders but decided to launch one more offensive against Reims with the ultimate objective of threatening Paris and drawing in Allied reserves. Foch again gained advance information of the impending attack and made adequate preparations – even beginning a bombardment of his own. Nevertheless, one of the attacking German armies made substantial progress and crossed the Marne. However, its progress was deceptive and the attackers encountered strong resistance at the second line of defence. Although, again, there was alarm in Paris, Ludendorff realized the strength of the forces now opposing him and on 17 July halted the attack, still hoping, despite the belief of many of his troops that they had been engaged in Champagne in the final *Friedenssturm*, that the time was ripe for the Flanders campaign. However, the loss of morale among German troops was becoming apparent – the influenza outbreak over the previous few weeks had sapped many of them physically. And there was an even greater surprise in store which finally ended the Flanders dream.

On the morning of 18 July Foch ordered the counter-offensive to begin, with the objective of wiping out the German salient on the Marne. Tanks and infantry were used in successful combination and took advantage of surprise. The Americans joined in, Pershing at last able to form the First American Army. However, German forces safely recrossed the Marne and were able to regroup along the line of the river Vesle. Nevertheless, the salient had been eliminated and Foch was promoted to marshal of France on 6 August for his pains. German losses since the spring now amounted to some 800,000. The Allies sensed that they were in the ascendancy, though no collapse appeared imminent. It was decided to press ahead immediately with an attempt to reduce the Amiens salient. British, French, American and imperial troops, together with tanks and aircraft, took part in the successful onslaught on 8 August. German divisions reeled under the impact and some fifteen thousand German prisoners were captured. Ludendorff reported to the Kaiser that the German army had ceased to be a perfect fighting instrument. The Allies had a brief pause but on 21 August the offensive resumed on a much wider front. At the end of the month the Germans were back on the Hindenburg Line – their departure point five months earlier. The Amiens salient had been reduced. It was then the American turn to take the offensive – preceded by the customary argument between Pershing and Foch. In the end they attacked in Lorraine and cleared the St Mihiel salient in four days by mid-September.

It was now time to think in terms of master-plans which might end the war, though there remained a presumption that the campaigning would extend into 1919. Foch himself thought it might end earlier if he could disrupt the vital railway line running from Lille to Strasbourg. If he could capture certain crucial junctions the Germans would have difficulty in receiving adequate supplies. Isolated, certain sections of the German army could be defeated in a piecemeal fashion. Even if the bulk of it nevertheless succeeded in withdrawing into Germany, it would be compelled to leave a great deal of equipment behind. If all went well, Foch hoped to accomplish a pincer movement, with a Franco-British force attacking from the north-west and a Franco-American from the south. Belgian, Italian and Portuguese contingents would also join the attack. The German forces were now numerically inferior and about a quarter of their available divisions were under strength. Foch intended to throw as many different units into action in as many different places as possible.

The attack began in the south on 26 September as Franco-American forces struck in the direction of Mézières and Sedan. Three days later British, French, Canadian and Belgian forces attacked in the north-west. The co-operation between the armies in both of these attacks was excellent. However, criticism of the disappointing progress made by the Americans began to be heard. It was very easy to describe them as inexperienced and their casualties were particularly heavy. In fact, the attack in the north-west encountered comparable problems and progress in Flanders was slow. The Germans took advantage of their fortified positions to fight furiously but an increasing despondency on their side could not be disguised. The initiative was clearly with the Allies and in October they steadily consolidated their advance, unspectacular though it was. At this juncture, political calculation and military strategy increasingly intermingled. The Allied advance had not been as great as had been anticipated. The Germans were not surrounded and the natural obstacles to campaigning in Flanders in the winter were as great as ever. It did begin to look as though fighting would have to be resumed in 1919 if a substantial Allied military victory was to be achieved. By this point, however, Ludendorff had already decided that Germany would be best served by the conclusion of an armistice. There was a change of chancellor in Germany and President Wilson was informed in early October that Germany was prepared to negotiate for a peace on the basis of his Fourteen Points. Just over a month later, on 11 November, the armistice was signed.

Ludendorff's recommendation that Germany should seek an armistice was based as much on developments elsewhere as on the German position on the Western front. While that was grave, it was not yet catastrophic, but Austria-Hungary, Bulgaria and Ottoman Turkey were in dire straits. Germany's allies had all been expected to play their part in assisting the spring offensive in the West by their own efforts. Berlin would have liked Italy to be knocked out of the war so that Vienna could provide reinforcements for the Western front – German troops had already been withdrawn from the Italian front. In mid-June, with a small numerical superiority, the Austrians attacked the Italians and the five Franco-British divisions which had not been transferred back to the Western front. Perhaps because, in effect, two uncoordinated assaults were launched, they proved disappointing. One army briefly established itself across the river Piave but was then driven back after fierce fighting. The Italians crossed the river themselves but their commander resisted the temptation to mount his own offensive. Diaz wished to regroup and launch his major assault at a time of his own choosing. He was encouraged by reports that Austria-Hungary was on the point of internal collapse. The attack was launched on 24 October – a year after the humiliation of Caporetto. The intervening months had been used for intensive preparations and Diaz had 57 divisions under his command including, for the first time, an American contingent. This initial fighting was fierce – the Austro-Hungarian forces were not as demoralized as had been assumed – but gradually the Italians pushed more and more troops across the Piave and, after an intense struggle in the last few days of the month, the Austrian resistance crumbled and about half a million prisoners were taken. On the other hand, some South Slav soldiers fought strongly to the end, apprehensive about Italian ambitions in the Adriatic. An armistice was signed on 4 November. The Italians had regained their military self-respect by their victory at Vittorio Veneto, although some of their Allies wanted this offensive to have come rather earlier.

The defeat of the Habsburg forces was not the only disaster. In July 1918 General Franchet d'Espérey was appointed commander of the Allied forces in Greece and began to make preparations for an attack northwards which would coincide with the Allied offensive in France. French and Serb divisions attacked on 15 September and, within days, the Bulgarians were retreating. Cavalry units covered nearly one hundred miles in a fortnight. In the last few days of the month, an armistice was discussed and then agreed. The army was to be demobilized and the country was at the disposal of the Allies for their future operations. The Serbs advanced through their own country and Franchet d'Espérey marched across Bulgaria and entered Romania shortly before the war came to an end. It was a modest achievement for an army of 350,000 men whose presence had not disturbed the supply line between Germany and Turkey for the duration of the war. And Bulgaria, by itself, had never been likely to tip the balance of the conflict.

In this final episode, British action had been concentrated against Turkey and formed part of a many-sided envelopment of the Ottoman empire. The capture of Jerusalem had been followed by the usual debate between those in London who believed that a further advance to Aleppo would lead to the collapse of the Turkish war-effort and those who believed it would not and who felt, in addition, that troops could not be spared for such a purpose, given the gravity of the position in France. The decision was taken to transfer troops from Mesopotamia and in the spring Allenby assembled his forces, only to find that he had to sacrifice a considerable number of men for France. The Turks, aided by a small German force, were now commanded by Liman von Sanders. The encounters between the opposing forces were inconsequential – the British imperial forces became accustomed to crossing to and fro over the Jordan. Lawrence, meanwhile, refined his raiding tactics and finally succeeded in making the Hejaz railway useless and cutting off Medina. It was not until September that the imperial forces and their Arab allies were able to break through. The battle of Megiddo, fought in mid-September, was the best kind of victory – it was achieved with comparatively little fighting. Damascus was reached by British and Arab forces on 1 October in what was now a rapidly-moving campaign. Different units speedily captured the important towns – Beirut, Homs and finally, on 26 October, Aleppo. Mustafa Kemal still hoped to make a stand north of the city but it proved impossible to check the British advance – tired though the troops were after travelling some 500 miles in just over a month. Turkish resistance was effectively at an end and an armistice between Britain and Turkey was signed on 30 October. This act did not prevent the Turkish commander at Mosul threatening to continue the fight when British troops appeared before the city on the following day. A few days later, however, he bowed to the inevitable. Indian, Australian, British and New Zealand forces seemed to have secured the supremacy of the British empire in the Near East. Peace, in this sense, had arrived, though that did not prevent the continuance of skirmishing on a considerable scale in such regions as Armenia and Georgia where there were ample local ingredients for continuing conflict.

Such unsettled conditions did not only obtain in the Middle East. German Baltic barons showed no great disposition to believe that the war had come to an end. Nor did the intrepid Lettow-Vorbeck in East Africa. In ignorance of wider developments, he captured a small Northern Rhodesian town two days after the armistice had been signed in France. When this further development was drawn to his attention he agreed, after due deliberation, to surrender, concluding that to reverse the verdict in Europe might tax even his ingenuity.

3 Modes of Warfare

Combined operations, the conscious welding together of land, sea and air activity in a co-ordinated plan, scarcely existed between 1914 and 1918. The Dardanelles operation was a conspicuous example of inadequate consultation. The British raid on Zeebrugge in April 1918, even though it was not a complete success in its objective of blocking the exit from the harbour, did give a glimpse of what an amphibious operation, with air support, might achieve. If full-scale joint planning was rarely attempted, the First World War was nevertheless the first major struggle in which all three modes of warfare were significant. It was also a contest which increasingly hinged upon scientific discovery and application, upon industrial capacity and upon intelligent use of manpower. The 'Home front' became almost as important as the scenes of actual battle. The ability to fight rested upon all of these interlocking factors. No belligerent could afford to show serious shortcomings in any major department of warfare, though in particular aspects the balance of advantage was constantly shifting. There was a continual race to perfect both new weapons and counter-measures that would neutralize their importance.

Land

Massive armies remained the focus of popular interest and attention. The outcome of the war would be determined by the battles between them. At this juncture, Europeans could reasonably claim that they led the world in military organization. The task of supplying such enormous forces with equipment and provisions was a major endeavour in itself. The populations of European countries which military planners could tap far exceeded those of a century earlier. There was, however, a clear disparity between the Central Powers (Germany 70 million and Austria-Hungary 50) and the Allies (Russia 160 million, United Kingdom 46 and France 38). The other major relevant powers (the United States 96 million, Italy 35, as against the Ottoman empire 20) further contributed to the Allied numerical advantage. In addition, Britain and France could have access to colonial populations which exceeded those of the metropolitan countries. There were also the self-governing British dominions. Such round figures give a general indication of strength but their significance was reduced by a number of obvious factors. It was widely supposed that physical efficency and martial zeal mattered supremely. The belief in the capacity of their forces shown by German military planners and commanders was an important aspect of their willingness to risk conflict. Naturally, too, there were different opinions about the proportion of a country's population which could be mobilized without serious consequences for industrial or food production.

In August 1914, the Russian army was the largest, with a force of over 1 million men, followed by Germany with some 850,000, France with some 700,000, Austria-Hungary with some 450,000 and Britain some 250,000. What was crucial, however, was how many trained men could be speedily mobilized and, while like cannot exactly be compared with like, the Russian figure then goes up to 5 million, the German to 4½, the French to 4, the Austro-Hungarian to 3 and the British to 1. Of the smaller states initially involved, Belgium could mobilize over 100,000 and Serbia 200,000. When they came into the war Italy could mobilize 1,250,000 men and Romania 290,000. Portugal and Montenegro had very small forces. Bulgaria's standing army was about the same size as Romania's. The armies of Ottoman Turkey and the United States stood at some 200,000.

Attention to the total number of men mobilized reinforces the point that the composition of the armies of 1914 was very different from those of 1918. The later lack of glamour in their uniforms is also indicative. Russia mobilized 12 million, Germany 11, France just over 8 and Austria-Hungary just under, the British empire nearly 9, Italy 5½, the United States 4½, Ottoman Turkey nearly 3, Bulgaria over 1. Circumstances were against the expansion of the Belgian army, but Romania and Serbia each mobilized some three-quarters of a million. Among the major powers, France mobilized the largest proportion of her population. New Zealand, however, sent abroad over 100,000 men out of an estimated 250,000 of military age. Some 6 million men went to war in 1914 and by its close around ten times that number had taken part in it. These new soldiers were normally fitted into old regiments and divisions. Death and expansion frequently changed their actual character, although the attempt was made to preserve the essence of prewar codes and conventions. The assimilation of such numbers into coherent and disciplined units remained a major preoccupation of their commanders throughout the war, though many of them were inevitably new soldiers themselves.

The assumed need to mobilize such forces had involved all European states in complex issues of civil–military relations. Socially and politically, armies were conservative institutions, closely linked to the established order in the monarchies of Europe. All armies experienced a tension between the demands of professionalism and the need for cohesion and shared values in the officer corps. The army, it was argued, was still the school of the nation but military planners oscillated between their fear that a precious ethos would be diluted and a desire to increase the army's size and influence. 'Militarism', the pre-eminence of military values and requirements, was for historical reasons especially characteristic of Prussia/ Germany, and its political and military classes closely interpene- trated each other, but that condition was not confined to Central Europe. In Italy the army saw itself as the embodiment of national unity, still only precariously established. In France, republicans feared that the expansion of the army without its 'purification' might threaten the stability of the Third Republic. The political and reli- gious views of intending officers were not irrelevant and professional competence could not be the sole criterion for promotion. For several decades, the major European states had wrestled with their military service legislation. Political pressures pointed in the direction of restricting or removing the ability to purchase exemption or substi- tution, but exemptions or anomalies continued to exist. In France, however, exemptions had been virtually eliminated and, in circum- stances of political controversy, military service was extended from two to three years in 1913. Russia had recovered with amazing faci- lity from the setback of the Russo-Japanese war and a 'Great Pro- gramme' being pushed through on the eve of war had as its objective a peacetime army three times the size of the German. Inevitably, it seemed, it was always the German army with which comparison was made throughout Europe. Yet, at least in comparison with Russia, the German military authorities were not satisfied with the army apportionment and were irked by the restrictions placed by the Reichstag. Her military traditions were intact but there were some who feared that Germany was in danger of being squeezed by Russian numbers and the sheer intensity of French training. On the eve of war in France 85 per cent of the relevant age group were trained, but only 50 per cent in Germany. The United Kingdom was unique in not having a system of military service, though in the years before the war there was an unsuccessful campaign for its introduction. Nevertheless, when he was war secretary, Haldane attempted to develop both a Territorial Force and an Officers' Training Corps. Even so, Britain remained distinctly unmilitary in comparison with the continent. There was no pressure from the Left in Britain for a 'new army' comparable with the contemporary views of French socialists.

There was no doubt that armies were expensive. It seems possible that military expenditures were reaching a level in 1914 beyond which even the most autocratic regime could not go. In what was once more a reflection of numerical inferiority, France was spending about a third of her budget on the army in the years before 1914. Russian military expenditure had been steadily rising and seemed poised to go beyond even that proportion. The German proportion was a little less, though in real terms it amounted to more than was being spent by France. The Austro-Hungarian figure was also high – and it was sustained with more difficulty. However, no government doubted its responsibility to 'modernize' the armed forces. Underdeveloped countries were eager to enlist the expertise of the advanced countries. The Ottomans, for example, gained German advice and money for their army, which they attempted to balance by obtaining British naval guidance. Not for the last time in such relationships, the advice was appreciated but the accompanying arrogance was disliked. Inevitably, therefore, armaments was a big and highly competitive industry, with ramifications throughout the economy. Marder has estimated that perhaps one-sixth of the British workforce depended on Royal Navy contracts in 1913. Critics of the armaments industry called the manufacturers 'merchants of death' and professed to detect their influence behind the scenes, fomenting international discord for the sake of profit. There is little evidence that this was the case. On the other hand, it is possible to see in the connexions between some manufacturers and governments a prefiguring of a later 'industrial-military complex'. These industries, however, were not autarkic in a way that would be expected if a clear national strategy was evident. In 1914, for instance, British manufacturers had hastily to try to find alternative supplies of vital phosphorus and optical glass, having relied hitherto on German sources. In Italy neither businessmen nor military men correctly anticipated each other's needs.

The problems involved in supplying these huge forces were formidable. The basic necessity was food for men and beasts, but fundamental needs were accompanied by a host of ancillary requirements. By 1918, the supplying of the British army in France had become a sophisticated and intricate operation. French ports, in particular, were much affected by the demands of war. Rouen, Le Havre, Bordeaux and Marseilles all recorded substantial population increases. At least in Western Europe, the railway networks enabled sufficient material to be moved close to the front but there were great difficulties in trying to keep the railheads sufficiently near an army on the move. The size and weight of the German army in 1914 may have been too great for the available transport. The needs of all armies steadily mounted as the war continued. Van Creveld notes that in 1914 a British division required 27 wagon loads of supplies of all classes per day. Two years later, food and fodder required 20 loads and combat material 30 loads. About half a million shells, for example, were brought up for the British offensive on the Somme in 1916. In this and other instances, however, material on such a scale could not be rapidly moved to suit the whim of a commander – despite the growth in motor transport. It may go too far to suggest that strategy was 'an appendix of logistics' but its scope was certainly much reduced.

The sound of gunfire scarcely ever ceased. The artillery provided the bass notes and did most of the damage, despite an initial French calculation, derived from the Russo-Japanese war, that losses would be caused to 85 per cent by small arms. The French 75mm gun proved superior to the German 77mm, but that advantage was offset by the devastating impact of the German howitzer. The static nature of the war encouraged the virtually permanent siting of these enormous pieces of equipment; something which, in turn, reinforced that lack of movement. Engineers worked frantically to improve the performance of guns, and gunners mastered new techniques in their use. Improvements in the calibration and location of guns allowed more accurate fire and permitted infantry to reach their objectives before the enemy could respond. These highly complex fire plans required central co-ordination and specialist advice. The acme of the art was counter-battery shooting. The Germans held the ascendancy in artillery power until the middle of the war when the Allies caught up. There was probably nothing more frightening in the war than a sustained artillery barrage.

From the standpoint of the infantry, these massive pieces were awesomely distant. What they relied upon for their own defence were the rifle and the grenade. For both sides, rifles were the essential companion pieces, to be cosseted for the duration, but skill in the use of a Lee Enfield varied enormously, and in conditions of trench warfare the opportunities for use were less frequent than might be supposed. That was not true of the grenade, which could be lobbed with greater impunity. Initially, German grenades were superior, but British types improved both in design and performance. What brought a new dimension, however, was the relatively light machine-gun, the Lewis. One of its advantages was that it could be carried easily in an advance. A strong and skilled performer could fire 550 rounds in a minute and the presence of a cluster of such guns could be reassuring for a battalion, so long as they did not jam. Its conspicuous consumption of ammunition was, by the same token, a source of operational difficulty. The accuracy of machine-guns was frightening. They could be fired with mathematical precision, and at night if need be. It is somewhat futile to try to determine whether artillery or the machine-gun was the more important land weapon; both played their destructive parts. In contrast to the various types of machine-gun, the mortar was a simple weapon, capable of firing off shells with speed and great accuracy. These weapons were not new when war broke out, though the scale of their use and effectiveness had not been widely predicted. Both sides struggled to gain permanent mastery in 'the new warfare' but its dynamics proved beyond the control of anyone. Even the expectations engendered in some quarters by the development of gas and tanks were not fully realized.

Chemical warfare seemed to offer endless possibilities. Physicists and chemists were recruited and urged to put their knowledge to good use on the pretext that countless lives could be saved by drawing the war to a speedy end. Brains which later gained Nobel Prizes (and even a Stalin Prize) busied themselves on the notion. Tear gas was first used at the beginning of 1915 but it was the use of chlorine by the Germans at Ypres on 22 April which caught the headlines and was denounced as a violation of the laws of war. So delighted was the Kaiser at the effectiveness of the cloud gas in opening a gap in the French lines, and the early German advance through it, that he promised the soldier brother of one of the chemists a bottle of pink champagne. It did not take long to improve on chlorine and to use shells and mortar canisters rather than cylinders. It was the French who pioneered the use of shells for, despite their denunciation of German initiative, the Allies reciprocated. The use of phosgene was followed by mustard gas – the most effective and widely used gas by the end of the war. Yet, despite the alarm and panic initially caused, it did prove possible to introduce face masks and other devices which reduced the impact of chemical warfare, though never completely eliminating it. The German decision to use chlorine at Ypres had been contentious in military circles. 'War has nothing to do with chivalry any more,' one German general wrote to his wife, 'the higher civilization rises, the viler man becomes.'

The clumsy ungainly fabrication called a tank seemed, in comparison, less odious, though certainly not pleasant to encounter. The idea of a bullet-proof machine had an obvious appeal, particularly as a way of breaking the domination of the machine-gun. Separately, the British and the French experimented with various types, but the forward leap in technology required to produce efficient versions was considerable. Sceptics abounded. The unreliability of early models was notorious. Their offensive potential was glimpsed but could not be realized. The performance at Cambrai seemed to point the way but the mauling suffered by French tanks a few months earlier at the hands of German heavy machine-guns was a reminder that there was still a long way to go. Of the belligerents, however, it was only the British and French who produced them on any scale. The German tanks were a failure and a considerable body of German opinion was inclined to rely on the increasingly successful anti-tank tactics.

All at Sea

In the decade before 1914, it had been the naval race which caught the headlines in the increasingly significant and widely read press. The technological advances of the late nineteenth and early twentieth centuries transformed the capacities and naval plans of the major maritime powers. There was general agreement that naval strength was a vital aspect of national well-being, neglected only at peril. It was the arrival of the Dreadnought which simultaneously excited enthusiasm and apprehension. 'We want eight and we won't wait' was a British jingle which had its equivalents elsewhere in the world. As first sea lord after 1904 Fisher showed ruthless zeal and technical expertise in pushing through the new programme in the confident belief that thereby the Royal Navy would rule the waves and justify the national expenditure upon its equipment. He showed an egocentric flair in cultivating the necessary political and press contacts to ensure that the Royal Navy remained the darling of public opinion. The naval hierarchy stuck firmly to the view that Britain was a maritime power and was only reluctantly drawn into accepting that it had a role in support of a British army which might actually fight on the European mainland. There was, indeed, no disputing that the United Kingdom was an insular power and that it posssessed some 11½ million tons of merchant shipping – more than twice that possessed by the other initial belligerents put together. It was only appropriate that the Royal Navy should be the largest in the world – with some 65 battleships and 120 cruisers (not to list destroyers and many more smaller craft). It was very conscious of being the 'senior service', yet pride in its past complicated the attitude of admirals to the revolution in gunnery, ship design and strategy through which they were living. The tactics employed by Nelson at Trafalgar still excited undue interest. Nevertheless, important reforms in recruitment and education for officers and men left little doubt among contemporaries that Britain had the ships and the men. Churchill argued that it would be wrong and unwise to trade indefinitely on the sense of discipline and loyalty possessed by sailors. Some admirals detected evil results from the 'mischievous socialistic literature' reaching the lower decks. The activities of socialist speakers on the promenade at Weymouth was a particular cause for concern. It remained to be seen whether the British could fight effectively in the major encounters between battle fleets that were anticipated.

The Royal Navy's re-equipment had been accelerated by the challenge presented by the growth of the Imperial German Navy. It was only reasonable, it was claimed, that Germany should have a navy capable of protecting her growing overseas trade. Tirpitz, with full support from the Kaiser, was prepared to mount a challenge and risk confrontation. If that seemed foolhardy, indeed pointless, given a context in which it was likely that Germany might be supporting Austria-Hungary against France and Russia, the navy had an important social function. It was conceived as a genuinely imperial force, *the* expression of the Wilhelmine era. It would appeal to the commercial classes. Its construction would provide employment and retard the advance of dark democratic forces. Frustrated though he was in some of his schemes, Tirpitz could display a fleet of 40 battleships and 57 cruisers in 1914.

The other European powers were also enthusiastically building, or rebuilding, their navies. Trying to escape from the humiliation of the Japanese war, in the years before 1914 the Russian navy was optimistic. Vast programmes of expenditure had been drawn up for the navy, latterly about half that for the army. There were ambitious plans on the drawing boards though, as in so many other aspects of Russian life, there was a puzzling disparity between the modernity of the schemes under way and the backwardness of existing provision in certain departments. The ratings were conscripts serving for five years – only 5 per cent in the Baltic fleet were career sailors. The attitude of their officers towards these men was frequently contemptuous. The structure of command and the lack of up-to-date naval regulations did not make for confidence. Even so, Russia went to war with around a dozen battleships and a dozen cruisers. The battleships were pre-Dreadnought – the Dreadnoughts were laid down and it remained to be seen how speedily they could be finished. The French attached a good deal of importance to the Russian fleet, partly because their own naval preparations did not compare with their military. In 1914 France possessed 28 battleships (only 2 of which were Dreadnoughts of the most modern class) and 34 cruisers. Although frequently not considered a naval power, Austria-Hungary had a fleet which was only slightly smaller (and marginally more modern) than that of Russia. Japan remained determined to keep in the forefront of naval development. Convinced of the inexorable logic of bigness, the Japanese naval attaché in London took the initiative in persuading his government that a battleship being built for Japan by Vickers should have 14-inch guns – then unknown in the Royal Navy. The Italian navy was not going to be left out of the race – expenditure on the navy rose at a much faster rate than on the army. By 1908 Italy was spending twice as much as Austria-Hungary on its navy, though she did not reap twice as much benefit. The United States navy too was rapidly developing into a major fleet, capable of sustaining operations both in the Pacific and the Atlantic. American ship-building capacity was such that American admirals saw little reason for the United States to accept British naval superiority for much longer. In all those countries at this time there was a certain glamour about big ships and there was less opposition from the Left to naval as opposed to military expenditure, perhaps because Dreadnoughts were less useful for controlling street demonstrations.

Mere numbers, however, are not very revealing. The effectiveness of armaments and armour had yet to be fully tested and much could depend upon the deployment of the fleets. The Russians tried, not very successfully, to decide whether operations in the Baltic or the Black Sea would be most important. Because of the recent understandings with Britain, the French were able to concentrate their fleet in the Mediterranean. Italy and Austria-Hungary planned their operations in terms of a struggle for control in the Adriatic. Japan and the United States devised their programmes primarily in relation to each other and the Pacific. The Royal Navy had been drawn more and more into considering the defence of the United Kingdom, but remained world-wide in its depositions. It was aided, as appropriate, by the small but modern navies of the dominions. Colonies and coaling stations also gave Germany an ability to operate globally, though with less facility. Yet, despite the impressive national displays of strength, it was impossible to judge how the fleets would fare in battle and how vital mastery of the seas would prove.

On the surface, there could be nothing more impressive than these mighty vessels of upwards of 20,000 tons, capable of 20 knots and of firing at a range of some 10 miles, but it was below the surface that the problem lay. The decade before 1914 saw the proliferation of submarine manufacture. The French and, to some extent, the Americans were the pioneers in design and development, encountering many difficulties *en route*, not to mention some disasters. Enthusiasts waxed lyrical on their potential but to others they looked puny beside the Dreadnought. Germany started late, but learnt from the mistakes of others. The German U-boats from 1907 were conceived as having an oceangoing rather than a coastal role. The British still wavered on this point but took a lead in the use of diesel engines. The Germans, however, showed clear superiority in periscope design and construction. On the eve of war, there was little to choose between the most advanced class of British and German submarine in terms of speed, but the latter could travel further. In 1914, even Russia had a few more submarines than Germany (Britain and France had both about three times as many), but it soon became evident that this numerical disparity was meaningless since many of the Allied vessels were already obsolete. It was unclear what impact this new capability would have on war at sea. Balfour confessed to

Fisher in 1913 that he was worried about the capacity of the enemy's submarine to 'render *our* position untenable'. Indeed, the sinking of three British cruisers, the *Aboukir*, *Hogue* and *Cressy* on one day by a single U-boat in September 1914 seemed to justify such fears. However, admirals were reluctant to think that sweeping changes were in the offing, though it was recognized that the coincidental developments in torpedoes posed a serious threat.

It was not the submarine which caused initial gloom and despondency but rather the activities of German cruisers in the Mediterranean, the Pacific and the Indian Ocean. The daring of such ships as the *Karlsruhe* and the *Emden* had not been anticipated. They were faster than their British counterparts and their guns were more effective. The battle of Coronel in November 1914 was a British defeat, only redeemed by the success of the battle of the Falkland Islands the following month. These were exciting encounters, but hardly the meeting between the major battle fleets which it was frequently thought would have an early and decisive impact on the outcome of the war. The British Grand Fleet was on station blocking the exit into the Atlantic between Scotland and Norway and the Channel Fleet blocked the entrance to the English Channel at the straits of Dover. The general German expectation was that the Grand Fleet would have advanced to blockade the Heligoland Bight, where the German High Seas Fleet occupied a well-defended corner. If a battle ensued, the Germans might well suffer heavy losses. If they did not emerge to fight, the British would have gained naval mastery. Instead, both sides sent underwater flotillas to find out what was happening, the German U-boats inflicting more damage and panic in the process. The alarm caused by the possible presence of submarines led both sides to show extreme caution and refrain from adventures. Such engagements as did take place, for example the battle of Dogger Bank in January 1915, only involved a small number of ships. The High Seas Fleet stayed at home for the rest of the year but early in 1916 its new commander, Admiral Scheer, planned further raids and actions in the hope of being able to deal separately with the battle-cruiser fleet at Rosyth before the Grand Fleet, stationed at Scapa Flow, could be brought to give support. Planning such an enterprise was not helped by the British ability to read German wireless signals. Nevertheless, on the last day of May 1916 there were the ingredients for an enormous and possibly conclusive contest. When the opposing scouting ships first made contact the British were not aware that the High Seas Fleet was at sea and the Germans were not aware of the presence of the Grand Fleet. Nevertheless, a battle of a kind was arranged off the Jutland Bank. It proved a sufficiently enigmatic encounter for both sides to be able to draw some satisfaction from the outcome. The British force was superior but it suffered more substantial losses and the High Seas Fleet got away. The battle cruisers, successful at the Falklands and Dogger Bank, proved a disappointment. Acutely conscious, as they believed, that they could lose the war in an afternoon, the British were a little too cautious. In retrospect, the course of the battle has been meticulously scrutinized but it remains a baffling mixture of bad luck, bad communications and indifferent judgement at vital points. The engagement taught the British that, piece for piece, neither their ships nor their shells were superior. However, with the exception of another outing in mid-August and a sweep in April 1918, the High Seas Fleet did not again take the initiative. Discontent among the inactive German crews grew. A mutiny had to be put down in August 1917 and the following year, at the very end of the war, there was another which was successful, though in the context of a crumbling Germany. It could be said that the British had held off the German challenge, though in doing so they tied up the huge resources represented by the Grand Fleet to little benefit. At least the Royal Navy did not mutiny.

By late 1916 it could be said with even more confidence that Allied naval superiority was overwhelming. The Russians did have several new Dreadnoughts and a group of cruisers available in the Baltic and a series of somewhat tentative encounters took place with no great consequence. They were a little more energetic in the Black Sea where the Turkish navy – of German ships – met its match. Six splendid Italian Dreadnoughts scurried in and out of Adriatic ports to no great purpose. Four splendid Austro-Hungarian Dreadnoughts did the same. It all seemed such an anti-climax and was largely put down to the unsporting activity of the submarine. In fact, apart from the uncertainty it engendered, the submarine was proving a disappointment to navies in the context of major naval operations. No U-boat sank or even hit a Dreadnought. Screened by destroyers, big battleships could make use of their speed to make themselves largely immune from attack. At the battle of Jutland the U-boats completely failed to play the part which Scheer had conceived for them. That is not to say, however, that in informal marauding activities the submarine's contribution was negligible. British E-class submarines, operating in the Baltic from Russian ports, caused the Germans considerable discomfort. The Germans caused the Russians anxiety in the Black Sea. The British upset the Turks in the Sea of Marmara. It was, however, the use of the submarine against commercial vessels that made a major impact on the course of the war.

If war came, it had been laid down before 1914 that Britain should do all in her power to prevent the continuance of German mercantile traffic and to confiscate all contraband bound for the enemy. A problem was that over the previous decade the British government had also been promoting international efforts to distinguish goods according to their importance and, in effect, to restrict the right to capture contraband at sea. It was only in the few years before 1914 that it was gradually realized that submarines and mines would make it impossible to maintain the alternative, a close blockade of the enemy's coasts and ports. A Declaration of London (1909) had been signed by the British government but not ratified. If its purpose was honoured it would be impossible for Britain to prevent or curtail imports which were going to neutral neighbours of Germany like the Netherlands. Trade in certain important commodities had indeed shown a mysterious growth. Deprived of its ability to trade by the British blockade off Scotland and in the English Channel, Germany made vigorous efforts to switch routes. On the other hand, if Britain developed a serious policy of economic warfare it would inevitably offend neutral states, most prominent of which was the United States. Illusory notions about German vulnerability in foodstuffs and certain raw materials made economic war seem an attractive option and it could be made more effective by enlarging the contraband categories (unilaterally), depriving Germany of certain commodities which were indeed of great importance. Russia and France were more than happy at such a prospect but American hostility was greatly feared in London. Attempts were made to mollify the United States whilst still making it possible to put pressure on the Scandinavian countries and the Netherlands. In an *ad hoc* manner, an elaborate machinery was evolved in 1915 which proved steadily more effective, though American hostility remained a problem. A ministry of blockade was set up in February 1916 to co-ordinate this activity and went beyond merely trying to prevent the shipment of contraband cargoes. The imports of certain neutral countries were, in effect, rationed by the British by referring to their prewar trade. Successful efforts, by one means or another, were also made to stop European neutrals from selling surplus products (including fish from the North Sea) to Germany. By the end of 1916, the cumulative effect of all these pressures has been called 'the most devastating, offensive use of sea power devised in the war'. It was true that the Germans showed great ingenuity in devising *ersatz* materials but even so some of the strains were beginning to show inside Germany. There were food riots and the 'turnip winter' of 1916–17 was to prove the worst of the war.

Since the Germans believed that what Britain was enforcing was itself *ersatz* international law, such inventiveness could be matched on their part by declaring in February 1915 that the waters around the British Isles constituted a 'War Zone'. British shipping would be sunk on sight and the safety of neutrals could not be guaranteed. Use of submarines for this purpose would necessarily mean that merchant vessels would be attacked without warning or regard for the fate of their crews. Vigorous protests from the United States led to some dilution in the application of this policy, but in May came the sinking of the *Lusitania* with the loss of over one thousand lives, 128 of them American. Partly because of the outcry that this action aroused, U-boat commanders were given restricted orders, particularly after the sinking of the *Arabic* in August. However, in 1915 submarines were responsible for sinking nearly three-quarters of a million tons of shipping. That winter, surface raiders also reappeared and caused considerable damage. In 1916 the German government could not make up its mind how far to risk alienating the United States by a vigorous use of the increasing numbers of U-boats at its disposal. Policy varied, with a lull in the summer following an active spring. In the autumn, restrictions were again lifted and nearly 150,000 tons of shipping went to the bottom in October. Britain and her allies could not replace losses on this scale. The admiralty tried to introduce new measures – additional minefields, nets and surface patrols – to stem the losses but less than 50 U-boats had been sunk by the end of 1916 and their numbers were steadily increasing. Allied shipping losses in 1916 were doubled from the previous year. There was no denying the gravity of the position but, from a German standpoint, the losses were insufficient. The blockade was biting, yet Britain was not crippled. One of Ludendorff's associates had spoken scathingly in the spring of the 'pinpricks' being administered by the submarines. Pressure mounted for the resumption of unrestricted warfare. After intense argument, that decision was agreed to, coming into operation from 1 February. It was hoped that Britain would be forced to make peace within five months and that would be before possible American intervention could bring relief.

There was deep pessimism at the admiralty in London. It looked as if the war at sea was going to be lost. Jellicoe, now first sea lord, felt that it was nearly too late to retrieve the shipping situation. Even the acceleration of the building programme and food rationing would not prevent disaster. Since it was probably impossible to prevent the U-boats from leaving their bases, they either had to be sunk at sea or there had to be protection for merchant ships. It was decided to concentrate on the former. The idea of the convoy was not sensible. The collection of ships, even under escort, made large losses likely and marshalling such a fleet would cause delays. It was also argued that steamships could not keep station in convoy. Finally, it was suggested that sufficient escorts were not available. Yet if an answer could not be found quickly, submission appeared almost inevitable. The Germans believed that losses of 600,000 tons per month would be sufficient and by April that figure had been comfortably exceeded. It dropped a little below in May, but rose again in June and July. It transpired, however, that the April losses were the highest. At the end of that month, Lloyd George paid a celebrated visit to the admiralty and insisted that the convoy system be given a trial, though possibly the admiralty itself was coming round to this view. Jellicoe himself was unconvinced, but a trial convoy for the United States set sail in late May, despite difficulties and mistakes. By mid-summer it became clear that the system was successful. It exposed the raider to counter-attack, prevented surface attacks in daylight and made it impossible to pick off ships at leisure. As the months passed, problems were ironed out and, although losses remained heavy, they no longer ran at crippling levels. It seems difficult in retrospect to understand the reluctance to try the system earlier, though the number of escort ships made available by the United States after its entry into the war in April is often overlooked. In the Mediterranean and the Atlantic, submarines continued to inflict heavy damage until the end of the war. Italy was perhaps even more vulnerable than the United Kingdom and in late 1917 submarine sinkings and shipping delays resulted in the importation for months of far less food, fuel and raw materials than were needed to keep the country going. That crisis too was eventually surmounted.

The submarine had therefore made its mark in a way which few anticipated in 1914. Its unrestricted use had come close to making it impossible for several Allied countries to continue the war. It should not be forgotten, too, that by the later stages of the war mines were proving extremely effective. British shortcomings in design and performance were initially conspicuous but by 1917–18 technical improvements were considerable. Many thousands of mines were laid, the most ambitious scheme being undertaken in 1918 to mine the 180 miles between Norway and Orkney. The fields laid in the Heligoland Bight added considerably to German problems. Yet, in the final analysis, the submarine had failed to deliver that knockout blow which its potential seemed to promise. The decision to use unrestricted submarine warfare, in so far as it precipitated the intervention of the United States, may even have lost Germany the war. On the other hand, the continuance of the British blockade and the sea power on which it rested did constitute a constant problem to Germany. Yet it was not decisive either, but one more facet of the multiplicity of pressures which constituted the waging of war. And technology produced one further twist: aircraft played an important part in convoy escort (and the Russians in the Black Sea showed great ingenuity in converting cargo ships to carry seaplanes). The British, too, had proper 'aircraft carriers' – a considerable change, since it was only just before the outbreak of war that an aircraft had first taken off from a ship. It was a recognition of the potential of flight.

Taking Flight

'I have not much news to-day,' wrote a young Englishman, not yet twenty, in 1917, 'except that I have had a splendid game of tennis, and a rather pleasant bombing raid.' The latter activity would not even have seemed possible when he was born. It was only in 1903 that the Wright brothers had managed to lift their flimsy structure off the ground. Four years later, in *The War in the Air*, H. G. Wells envisaged a devastating attack upon New York by a fleet of airships. In July 1909 Louis Blériot flew across the English Channel. A few months earlier, a sub-committee of the committee of imperial defence reported that although the invasion of Britain in airships was unlikely, the dropping of explosives and incendiary bombs could not be dismissed 'as an impossible operation of war'. Other observers felt that the likely progress of the science of aeronautics would be slow;

there was no need to get carried away. In Britain, steps were taken to improve aircraft design at the recently established National Physical Laboratory. There was considerable disagreement as to whether precedence should be given to the development of lighter-than-air or heavier-than-air craft. The Royal Flying Corps came into being in April 1912, with a naval and military wing. Pilots from both wings were to receive their training at a Central Flying School. Despite these developments in Britain, it was widely agreed that the initiative, both in technique and design, rested with the continental states. The Italians had even used aeroplanes in their war against the Turks in Tripolitania. The Germans appeared to place most hope in their rigid airships – Zeppelins. They could fly higher than aeroplanes and seemed suitable for carrying heavy loads of bombs, which could be dropped with precision. The French experimented both with balloons and aeroplanes. At the outbreak of war, Britain had a mere 37 planes while France had 136 and Germany 180, though too much weight should not be attached to these figures. It may be noted that by the close of the war France was building almost as many aircraft per day as she possessed altogether in 1914.

There was a great deal of experimentation and speculation in all the major belligerent countries, but no clear agreement on the use to which aircraft would be put. In Britain, the predominant initial view was that they would have a reconnaissance role, though Haig apparently doubted whether even this would be of significant value. The squadrons were, nevertheless, soon dispatched to France. Pilots speedily adapted themselves to their tasks – artillery spotting, photographic reconnaissance and the occasional piece of bombing. They sportingly carried rifles and revolvers in case any alien aircraft should chance to come near. The British stuck tenaciously to the view that aircraft should be maids-of-all-work, though it soon became apparent that different types were suited to different tasks. Even so, reconnaissance remained paramount and photographic skills improved with great rapidity, though it was by no means easy to make intelligent use of the information thus obtained. Flyers were regarded with some suspicion by soldiers on the ground since their ability to drop objects from the sky sometimes did not appear to be confined to enemy targets. Pilots and mechanics had to cope with a great many sudden emergencies. In the early stages of the war, mechanical unreliability was a greater hazard than the enemy.

If the reconnaissance function was proving useful, the obvious next step was to deprive the enemy of his information by shooting him out of the sky. The days when intrepid airborne cartographers excitedly waved at aliens similarly engaged did not last long. The problem with fighter aircraft was the propeller, which tended to get in the way when a pilot fired his gun at a target in front. He could even kill himself with his own bullets. The British were baffled, the French installed steel deflectors on the edge of each blade and the Germans, with the aid of a French aircraft which had fallen into their hands and a Dutch designer, Fokker, designed a gun whose rate of fire was itself controlled by the propeller. Temporarily, the Germans had an enormous advantage until the Allies learnt the secret from a captured German plane and did likewise. In general, however, the Germans were technically one step ahead, whether in the provision of pressure petrol gauges or efficient speed or altitude recorders. And they had their Zeppelins, though there was no plan for a specific air campaign as part of the general war plan. They too were divided between the navy and the army. The latter were used in France and Belgium in the first month of the war and there was general satisfaction at the accuracy of their bombing missions against military targets. There was less satisfaction at the number of Zeppelins lost in the process. The British also carried out a series of raids, the most successful of which was the attack on the Zeppelin base at Friedrichshafen in November 1914. Although daring, there was no possibility of being able to carry out sustained attacks. The objective of these strikes was to try to prevent Zeppelin attacks on Britain, but the first took place in January 1915. It was not very successful, but in May there were raids both on Southend and London causing civilian casualties and damage to property. Anti-aircraft guns and searchlights were hastily installed, but considerable fear remained. Over the next couple of months, several Zeppelins were brought down by British pilots and the anxiety lessened.

On the Allied side, the potential scope for bombing operations moved to the forefront. Much discussion centred on how bombing could be more accurate. As things stood, there were obvious inadequacies in equipment, training and operational methods. One report prepared for Flying Corps headquarters in June 1915 stated that over the previous four months there had been 141 bombing raids on railway stations in enemy territory in which nearly a thousand bombs were dropped. It appeared that only three raids were at all successful. Although bomb-sights were improved, advocates of long-range bombing had a hard time in such circumstances. They also had difficulties because to develop any semblance of a strategic air policy challenged the assumption by the army that air operations were merely an adjunct to the war on the ground. The army already resented the activities of the Royal Naval Air Service. Jurisdictional disputes took up a good deal of time and energy. Those who supported the idea of a substantial bombing campaign which might hit German industrial targets usually only did so with the proviso that nothing should be done to upset the requirements of the army on the Western front. That meant that very little was done in practice. The French Air Service was more adventurous and less constricted, though still on a modest scale.

It was the Germans who next took the initiative. By late 1916, the effectiveness of the Zeppelins had been reduced by improved British defences. Also, in one raid in October 1916 their vulnerability to high winds became apparent – one of the ships disappeared over the Mediterranean and was never seen again. A new twin-engined bomber, the Gotha, opened up new possibilities and intensive preparations were made over that winter. Raids on London and south-east England in May, June and July 1917 led to heavy loss of life and considerable damage to property. The attempt to intercept the bombers proved a complete failure. To add to the humiliation, the attacks on London took place in the daylight. L. T. Hobhouse, the political philosopher, was sitting in his Highgate garden annotating Hegel's theory of freedom at the time. His first reaction was to mock himself for theorizing when the world was tumbling about his ears. His second reaction was that in the bombing of London he had 'just witnessed the visible and tangible outcome of a false and wicked doctrine the foundation of which lay . . . in the book before me'. It was actually a comfort in such circumstances to know that his son was a pilot in France.

The cabinet, however, desisted from a consideration of the metaphysical theory of the state and turned, instead, to an exponent of holism, General Smuts, for some comfort. He speedily produced a report in August 1917 which stated clearly that the air service could be used 'as an independent means of war operations'. What Londoners had just seen might merely be the prelude to the future devastation of enemy lands, industries and towns. Within months, the government had accepted the need for a separate air service. The first Air Council came into being in January 1918 and the Royal Air

Force was formed on 1 April. There was no comparable separation of an air force on the continent. In the final months of the war, ambitious plans were developed for bombing raids into Germany, making use of the capacity of the Handley Page aircraft, which could carry a heavier load than the Gothas. In the event, most of these schemes were not carried out. Constant saturation bombing was a dream left for the future. Operationally, in the final months, it was the Germans who still showed an ability to innovate. In the March 1918 offensive they used air squadrons in support of the infantry offensive more effectively than had ever been done before. By this time, however, the Allies (with American support) had sufficient fighters to blunt the effectiveness of the initial assault. In the final stages of the war, the Allies had achieved air superiority – a concept which had little significance in 1914.

It was the promise rather than the actuality of air power which most struck contemporaries. The war had not been decided in the air. Nevertheless, the race for supremacy had produced astonishing developments in a short space of time. The general purpose plane had given way to a sophisticated set of types – the French Nieuport and Spad, the British Camel and the German Fokker, to name but a few fighters. It was grandiose to speak of aircraft factories in 1914, but not by the end of the war. Speed, range, and rate of climb increased, giving advantages first to one side and then the other. There were design dead-ends as well as breakthroughs. British machines were drearily khaki, but the Germans permitted the most colourful displays. Zeppelins, much feared at the beginning of the war, had largely lost their capacity to inspire terror at the end. Both sides were not altogether happy about bombing raids which led to civilian casualties. Qualms on this score were one reason for the failure to press on with the 'successful' bombing raids on London in the summer of 1917. The fact that such raids had occurred, however, gave a new dimension to war and called into question ancient distinctions between civilians and soldiers, combatants and non-combatants.

The aircraft themselves frequently had a short life. So, in many instances did their pilots; but it was a short and glamorous life. Their exploits in the skies took on a romance and excitement which was lacking in grim terrestrial encounters. The aeroplane, it was stated, was no mere mechanical contrivance but a triumph of man over matter. In this spirit the 'knights of the sky' waged their war. There was no manual for them as they struck out into the unknown. Each nation had its aces – William Bishop, Max Immelmann, Georges Guynemer, to name but a few. Baron Manfred von Richthofen was no better, to English minds, than the deadly Albert Ball. Perhaps the most exuberant flyers were the Italians in the Alps, their heads turned by thin air and mountains. Honour dictated that if an ace finally met his end his opponent should do his best to fly over and drop a wreath. In this mood, our youthful tennis-playing pilot also wrote that he thought 'the idea of dividing R.F.C. Squadrons up by public schools is splendid'. He added that, alas, it was impossible. Even flyers, it seems, had occasionally to come down to earth, though propagandists continued to make them seem superior to ordinary mortals.

It was a comfort to Lettow-Vorbeck in East Africa to know that a Zeppelin was seeking to reach him with necessary supplies.

4 Belligerent Aims

Grey, the long-serving British foreign secretary, gloomily took the view in late 1914 that for the duration of the war there was little that the foreign office could do. Diplomacy would be entirely subservient to military events. States would be guided in their dealings with each other by the fluctuating fortunes of battle. He was, perhaps, a little too pessimistic. As far as Britain was concerned, the handling of initially non-belligerent states like Bulgaria or the United States, of neutrals like Denmark or the Netherlands, or an ally like Japan could be of very great significance and did not hinge entirely on military factors. Nevertheless, the scope of foreign policy was generally very limited, at least until a late stage in the conflict. Whether reluctantly or with a good grace, foreign secretaries and foreign offices lost some of their political standing and frequently found new agencies and advisers usurping their role.

Every state had to have war aims and traditional bureaucracies played their part in formulating them. The status of a 'war aim' is, however, difficult to determine. Particularly in the case of Germany, some writers have seen in the early formulation of territorial and economic objectives confirmation of the expansionary pressures which thrust the country into war. Others have been more cautious, suggesting that once war had begun it was only natural to attempt to define objectives. To have aims in war was not the same as going to war for certain aims. It can be confidently stated that the shape of Europe and the world in 1919 did not correspond to the ambitions of any state which went to war in 1914. The formulation of war aims was a delicate task and, some said, a dangerous and unnecessary one. To enunciate specific goals might entail awkward commitments which it might be better to avoid. Failure to obtain them might appear a defeat. It was sounder to talk only in the most general terms and to concentrate the public mind upon victory as an end in itself. In public at least this was indeed the tendency in the early stages of the conflict. Detail was not completely absent but it was secondary – a shopping list would detract from the heroic character of the struggle. With the continuance of the war, however, this initial rhetoric proved inadequate. Articulate sections of public opinion claimed a right to know what their country was fighting for. Governments were wary of undue exposure because the objectives could then be subjected to cost-benefit analysis. They could be asked whether it was indeed worth the continued slaughter merely for the sake of 'x'. They might also be told that 'x' could in fact be obtained by negotiation with the enemy. And, indeed, the articulation of objectives was, from the side of governments, an initial counter in what might in the end turn out to be a bargaining process. The conspicuous display of what were conceived to be honourable objectives was also necessary in order to impress the United States. Even so, the precision of the public statements, and even more of the papers and memoranda that lay behind them, was spurious. Governments frequently did not know, at any given point, what they were fighting for. It was the fighting that mattered. The papers prepared by officials kept them happy and frequently had little relation to what was going on in the minds of their masters.

One further paradox soon became apparent, at least in the 'Anglo-Saxon' world. Many had persuaded themselves into fighting in the war because they professed to believe that only through fighting could war itself be banished. Here was no ordinary war for specific objectives, whether sordid or elevated. Here was a war against 'militarism', a war against war itself. It could not end in any ordinary fashion but had to be crowned by new institutional arrangements whose effect would be the abolition of international conflict: the League of Nations. There was no gainsaying the grandeur of this objective, but its very glory vitiated the possibility of compromise. To leave the 'international anarchy' intact by a patched-up peace settlement, even if that were possible, would only invite future conflict. A war aim on this scale was a formidable burden, though in fact it did not weigh too heavily with governments. The longer the war lasted, however, the more intolerable it became that it should not issue in something worthwhile.

German war aims were first formulated in the much-discussed 'November programme' of 1914, although drafts of the Kaiser's proclamation to the French people proved at least premature. The concept of *Mitteleuropa* loomed large. A customs and economic union between Germany and Austria-Hungary was advocated in various quarters as the basis for a new order in Central Europe. There were also ambitious plans, at the expense of France, Belgium and Portugal, for a German *Mittelafrika*, to which, in due course, Britain would be required to make a generous contribution from her African possessions. Bethmann Hollweg was determined that France should be so weakened by territorial adjustment and commercial and economic measures that she would never again become a great power. Belgium would lose territory, place her coast at German disposal for military purposes and, if allowed to continue as a state, would be reduced to a vassal of Germany. Luxemburg would become a German federal state. The Netherlands would be made internally dependent but could survive as far as externals were concerned. In the East, Russia was to be pushed back as far as possible and the non-Russian peoples were to be released from Russian domination. That might mean direct German control in the Baltic, in Russian Poland and, in the south, as far as the Crimea, or it could entail various forms of indirect influence. No doubt the details could be clarified in due course. Meanwhile, business and military circles became excited by the prospects. Most German political parties favoured an annexationist policy to some degree or other, including many socialists, though the latter tended to be keener on frontier changes in the east rather than west. They found that opposition to tsarism could justify their support. These objectives were not merely Prussian. The king of Bavaria wanted Alsace, though his ambition was contested by the grand duke of Baden. Belgium shorn of its degenerate Walloons was something that appealed to a number of princely houses.

Such heady goals were not merely the product of smoke-filled rooms after a good dinner. They were widely shared in German society, though there was disagreement as to whether *Mitteleuropa* and *Mittelafrika* could be simultaneously pursued and, if not, which was the wisest course. There were, however, certain snags, most conspicuously the future of Poland. It was a subject on which Vienna had decided views. The foreign minister of the monarchy saw the tentative German plans for the 'Congress' Poles as little more than direct annexation, with the antagonism this would cause amongst his own Poles. He had plans for an Austrian Poland. Nor, in general, were Austrian politicians and public enamoured of the concept of *Mitteleuropa*. 'The conquest of Austria is the most important German war aim' is how the Austrian economist Joseph Schumpeter reacted to Naumann's *Mitteleuropa*. It would be a Prussian-Lutheran-militaristic system which would shatter what he still believed to be the destiny of the Habsburg monarchy. The 'War aims of the Central Powers' was therefore something of a phrase, involving a good deal of dispute and ruffled feelings. Naturally, Vienna proposed that a settlement would have to remove the threat posed by the South Slav question, though there was disagreement between the two halves of the monarchy about the extent to which it entailed direct control over them. Albania, it was envisaged, would become a protectorate. Apart from the continuing dispute over 'Poland', the advent of Romania into the war in 1916 brought fresh problems, for there German economic and strategic interests were strong. In turn, Bulgarian aspirations in the Dobruja region proved contentious, though she sought her main territorial advantage at the expense of Serbia in Macedonia. Nor could Turkish views be ignored. It would be good to regain control of Egypt and Cyprus but, unfortunately for Berlin, there was unfinished business with Bulgaria. If it should come to a negotiated settlement, the Austrians tended to feel that German ambitions in the West were too extravagant, while the Germans did not detect any moderating of Austrian aspirations in south-eastern Europe.

It was President Wilson who first formally requested both sides to state in detail the peace conditions which they would accept. He had noted that hitherto, when couched in generalities, the terms had seemed the same. A few days earlier, in December 1916, the Central Powers had indicated a general willingness to negotiate. In doing so, there can have been little expectation that a settlement on the lines they had in mind would prove acceptable. It was conceivable, however, that a separate peace with either France or Russia could materialize. President Wilson would be pleased. Indeed, the relationship between London and Washington had been deteriorating for some months. Talk of a 'knock out blow' from Lloyd George in September had not been what the Americans wanted to hear. It did not seem to be in their interests for either side to gain a clear military victory. Suddenly, in the last few weeks of 1916, there seemed some room for diplomatic movement. Emperor Franz Josef of Austria died and there was also a change of foreign minister in Vienna. And in London there was a good deal of speculation about how the new prime minister would react and what interpretation was to be placed upon the American initiative. The extent of British financial and economic dependence upon the United States ensured careful attention to the problem. Britain and France had to stick together.

At this juncture, the aspirations which had undergirded their effort over two years did not have great significance. It was the Germans who occupied alien territory. Even to achieve a settlement on the status quo ante, they would have to make concessions. Not that the Allies would have been satisfied with that, even if it were obtainable. Initially, both Asquith and Grey had placed almost exclusive emphasis in their not very extended public statements upon the 'restoration' of Belgium. Grey placed great stress – though not all his colleagues agreed with him – on the need to minimize friction with the United States. He shied away from general undertakings about the future of Europe; nevertheless he found himself drawn into commitments by the exigencies of the struggle. The Treaty of London, which drew Italy into the war, explicitly promising her the Trentino, Trieste, Istria and certain parts of Dalmatia, represented a specific break (at the expense of Austria-Hungary) with the status quo. Also in the late spring of 1915 the Romanian government promised intervention, though not immediately, in return for very substantial gains, chiefly at the expense of Hungary. Attempts to entice Bulgaria were a failure. This was not surprising because of the 'knock on' effect of territorial adjustments already approved. Serbia was to receive Bosnia and Herzegovina, together with substantial access to the Adriatic.

By mid-1915 the pattern of commitments had already stored up trouble for the future. Britain, France and Russia appeared, even so, to be in general agreement on these schemes, yet the Western states were well aware of Russia's peculiar status in the area and the problems to which it might give rise. They were prepared, however, to make the symbolic concession of Constantinople and to recognize that Russia might exercise hegemony in the Balkans. The Russians themselves could not have put the matter with much more precision. Russian control in Constantinople did not please the Greeks and, of course, meant that the fate of the Ottoman empire had to be considered. The British talked rather generally about a federal state and did not favour partition but wanted Basra detached, and were in touch with certain Arab leaders, amongst whom was murmured the word protectorate. Already existing French interests in Syria meant that from October 1915 onwards the complex future of the Near East could only be tackled in conjunction with Paris, not always amicably.

Sir Mark Sykes negotiated for Britain, and his memorial brass on his estate in North Yorkshire suitably presents him in full armour. He and M. Picot then went on a crusade to Petrograd and, after adjustment, acquiesced in the proposed arrangements in return for a substantial slice of Anatolia. Grey noted a proposal in 1915 that Belgium should be given Palestine, but that was not serious. If the Allies had their way, the map of Europe would be as different from 1914 as it would be if the Central Powers had theirs.

The British did not enter into these arrangements with zest. They had joined in the bidding because of the need for allies and support. Particularly in relation to Italy's anticipated gains, elements in the foreign office and public opinion felt it risky, even offensive, to infringe the nationality principle. It might offer the only firm guide in the forthcoming territorial auction. The South Slavs, or at least those who claimed to speak for them, were already offended and might be alienated. Besides, to have soiled hands would prove awkward if there were a firm policy decision to seek the decomposition of Austria-Hungary on nationality lines. On that matter, the British had as yet taken no clear decision, though options had been kept open by encouraging the activities of certain self-styled Slav leaders and their supporters in London. It was no doubt heartening that some 90 per cent of Czechs resident in Britain volunteered for the British army, but their assistance would not be decisive. On the other side, it was an undoubted fact that British politicians showed no familiarity with the nationalities whose claims were so lauded in certain quarters. They had to take not untainted instruction from historians, among them H. A. L. Fisher, R. W. Seton-Watson and L. B. Namier. Lloyd George's fixed point was that the Serbs were like the Welsh. It did appear, though, that the rock of nationality could dissolve on inspection and, moreover, at least one minister found nationalism, whether Slav or Irish, obnoxious. The Easter Rising in Dublin was a reminder that for the British empire the principle was a two-edged sword. East-Central Europe without the Habsburgs would either be Russian or an unstable mess, conceivably both. Better to seek to detach the new emperor from German apron-strings by sustaining the integrity of his domain, adding the word autonomy for good measure. The contrary view was that such detachment was impossible. Suitably encouraged and controlled, the nationalities could disrupt the efficiency of the monarchy. If they were ignored, they might be bought off by Vienna. It was not forgotten in London that there were a lot of Poles with votes in the United States. Indeed, the presence of Poles everywhere was a problem.

In most of these arrangements made against the day of victory the British took the lead. Coal, manufactures and treasury loans gave London some leverage, providing proprieties were observed and Syria considered sacrosanct. French eyes were firmly fixed on Alsace-Lorraine, as her allies were informed immediately the war began. Since it was restitution, the predominant view was that not even a plebiscite would be required. Belgium, of course, should be restored. Grey made sympathetic noises, but the British made no public statement of support for the French aspirations in Alsace-Lorraine. Given their longer alliance and that they both saw themselves as land powers, it is not surprising that there was more argument on such matters between Paris and Petrograd than between London and Petrograd. The German presence in France diminished French concern about potential Russian expansion. Inevitably, the Russians appeared with their scheme for a Poland which would be under their direction and Paris remained non-committal about it. By 1916, however, the fate of Poland was causing difficulties between the two capitals. The French feared that the Poles might succumb to German blandishments and wished publicly to reassure them of their support for the Russian proposals. That smacked of interference in Petrograd. There was not, therefore, a straightforward division: France to do what she would in the West and Russia in the East. In fact, it was not certain what France did want in the West. The bland 'restoration' of Belgium disguised considerable impatience with Belgian aspirations, which could involve the annexation of Luxemburg. If the duchy was to go anywhere, it was preferable for it to come to France. Equally unresolved, though much debated, was the extent to which France should press territorial claims, for economic and strategic reasons, beyond Alsace-Lorraine.

It is against this background that the Franco-British reply to President Wilson on 10 January 1917 comes as no surprise. Washington was informed that Belgium and Serbia should be restored, French, Russian and Romanian territory evacuated and even, for good measure, 'the turning out of Europe of the Ottoman Empire as decidedly foreign to western civilisation'. The principle of nationality was alluded to, though in general terms – no specific reference to Poland, for example. There was also, for the first time, a recorded willingness to assist 'wholeheartedly' in creating a League of Nations to ensure peace and justice throughout the world. That, in turn, would enable land and sea frontiers to be guaranteed against unjustified attacks. President Wilson was thus given a clear indication of the Allied intention to fight on and left in no doubt that a League of Nations was not an alternative device for producing a settlement, but something which could only emerge from what the Allies regarded as a satisfactory peace. Contemporaneous Scandinavian attempts at mediation were firmly rebuffed. The Germans, a Danish emissary was told, had placed themselves beyond the pale and could only be treated as criminals. President Wilson did not agree. His first reaction was that the Allies were exaggerating and he spoke publicly on 22 January about the need to achieve 'peace without victory'. Other passages in the speech, however, could be taken to support an independent Poland and, obliquely, the restoration of Alsace-Lorraine to France. Wilson was annoyed that no German reply was forthcoming and the Franco-British reply was, to that extent, co-operative. However, German comments received in Washington at the end of January made it clear that Berlin still envisaged at least the subordination of Belgium. The German ambassador added that the terms were, in any event, out of date since they had been drawn up on the assumption that the Allies would accept the initial German peace offer. Within a couple of days, the ambassador further intimated the German intention to resume unrestricted submarine warfare on 1 February. President Wilson replied by breaking off diplomatic relations with Germany. Six weeks of exchanges had disclosed no basis for agreement.

The discussion of war aims, however, became something of a habit. The new British war cabinet found itself being supplied from various quarters with exciting plans covering the disposition of the entire globe. The proliferation of ideas makes it difficult to judge what weight ought to be attached to any of them at a time when bureaucratic hierarchies and procedures were particularly vulnerable. The same problem existed in France in early 1917. Elaborate efforts were made at this time to clarify understandings on Alsace-Lorraine and Poland respectively and something was put on paper. Within a couple of months, however, the Quai d'Orsay could not reconstruct what had happened and an incoming government disavowed the exchange of letters. The German government did not give any fundamental reconsideration to 'war aims' as such, being preoccupied with monitoring the progress of the submarine campaign and trying, not very successfully, to gauge American reactions. The flurry of British activity is chiefly to be explained by the increased pressure from the dominions. Lloyd George appreciated that if more men and materials were to be extracted, there would have to be at least symbolic consultations on peace terms. Such an exercise would inevitably bring up the problem of Japan.

Having declared war on Germany on 23 August 1914, the Japanese were in occupation of the German islands north of the equator, and in December informed the British that they intended to retain them. Having also subdued the German fortress of Tsingtao in Shantung, the Japanese presented the Chinese in the early months of 1915 with 'Twenty-One Demands' which started with the regulation of the position in Shantung province but which went much wider, referring to Manchuria and the appointment of Japanese advisers, the cumulative result of which would have been a virtual Japanese protectorate in China. The British government was acutely embarrassed. China was unstable, there was a European war on and the best that could be done was to persuade the Chinese in May 1915 to accept a modified version of the demands. Yuan Shih-k'ai, the ruler of China, found it increasingly difficult to maintain his position and, after his death in June 1916, warring factions re-emerged and no single government was discernible. The Japanese exploited the disarray and Britain's difficulties mounted. China still maintained diplomatic relations with the Central Powers but the steady increase in Tokyo's influence was unacceptable. On the other hand, as Grey reminded his colleagues, Japan had not given her initial support against Germany in the Far East without assurances that she could consolidate her hold on what she conquered. Otherwise, it would have been in Japan's interests to side with Germany and, indeed, both in 1915 and 1916 Germany made some attempts to persuade the Japanese to reverse their allegiance. If the Japanese could be persuaded to restrict their intentions to Manchuria and Fukien, a partial solution might then be to persuade the Peking government to join the war. That issue added to the already fierce divisions within China, but diplomatic relations with the Central Powers were broken off in March 1917 and war was declared on Germany in August. Some entertained the spectacle of millions of Chinese joining their new Allies in Europe. Balfour thought the idea 'idiotic' and 'insane'. Even if the situation in the Far East had temporarily eased, few British observers doubted that Japan, even though an ally, had every intention of using the European war to her own advantage. There were even some officials in the British India office who suggested that Japan turned a blind eye to the activities of Indian revolutionaries. 'We have to be prepared for Japanese hostility in a not remote future,' wrote one official in May 1916. The Indian CID went to considerable lengths to exercise surveillance over seditious groups with Japanese connexions – but it was not easy to determine the reality of the relationship. Fears of this kind were exacerbated because it was known that the Germans were also active in trying to foment disturbances in India, amongst other things trying to persuade the ruler of Afghanistan to invade. If not a battleground, therefore, the East none the less was a source of considerable concern. However, no serious action against Japanese control of German colonies could be contemplated since it was becoming apparent that Australia and New Zealand, who were most apprehensive about it, had every intention of retaining control over the colonies they had conquered. So did South Africa in German South West Africa. They were alarmed that a peace by negotiation might require them to forfeit these gains. It had become apparent that the 'war aims of the British empire' could not be solely based on the perceptions and interests of the United Kingdom.

If Asia caused deep concern amongst British policy-makers in the early months of 1917, the events that followed, the March and November revolutions in Russia and the entry of the United States into the war in April, transformed the context in which war aims had to be contemplated. The new Provisional government in Russia, under pressure, declared that it now favoured a settlement without annexations by force. Any new arrangements would have to be based on self-determination. Such a statement of principle was a significant change, though still susceptible of varied interpretation. Western governments were rather more concerned about the viability of the regime than about the precise implications of the new standpoint. However, the impact on some sections of British public opinion was considerable. Henderson, the Labour member of the war cabinet, visited Russia and returned with the conviction that it was essential to refashion Allied war aims to keep Russia in the war. There were plans for a conference of socialists at Stockholm, to be attended by delegates whose countries were at war. Henderson resigned from the cabinet when it reversed a previous decision to permit British attendance. In the event the Stockholm conference never took place, but the plans for it indicated a new mood. War aims now became much more a matter of public debate, although, for a few months, the Provisional government did abandon its attempts to revise war aims. The British League of Nations Society was formed in May 1917. It embarked on a vigorous programme of meetings and publications with the intention of persuading the government to go beyond mere endorsement of the League. Once detailed studies began, however, it became apparent that 'the League' could mean all things to all men. Some wanted a coercive organization, some wanted an international standing army, some wanted it to rely on economic sanctions, some wanted it to be open to all states while others wanted it restricted, at least in the first instance, to the Allies. One Labour document envisaged that it would possess important economic functions and that it would be the appropriate agency for the control of all European colonial territories in Africa and elsewhere. It would not be Germany alone which forfeited its imperial role.

The same shift of mood and expectation was discernible in France. In March, the new prime minister/foreign minister, Ribot, told parliament that France was not fighting a war of 'conquest', though there would have to be material guarantees of peace – which was taken to mean the kind of territorial expansion which the previous government had dabbled with. References to the League of Nations appeared over the next few weeks. Events in Petrograd produced divided counsels both on the spot and in Paris. The French ambassador thought anarchy was inevitable, though it might be delayed for a vital few months. But Albert Thomas, the socialist minister of armaments, formed the impression after his visit that if the Allies were prepared to 'jettison ballast' an upsurge of 'revolutionary patriotism' might yet be possible. Some French socialists now told the prime minister that they only supported the claim to Alsace-Lorraine based on its 1870 borders. Ministers reaffirmed their commitment to the more extensive 1790 borders but now kept silent on plans for the Saarland and the left bank of the Rhine. The Stockholm conference issue caused an even greater furore than it did in Britain. Secret sessions both of the chamber of deputies and of the senate discussed war aims in a fuller fashion than at any time since the outbreak of war. Throughout the summer some French socialists tried to extract from ministers statements about what precisely had been agreed in the past with Russia and what the present status of such undertakings was. Yet mystery still shrouded

French aspirations for the Rhineland and the Saar. However, by early autumn, with the Provisional government manifestly waning, it was becoming obvious that Russian assistance in winning the war was coming to an end. Since it was only from that quarter and not from the Anglo-Saxon world that support for such annexation had been sought it looked perforce as though this dream might have to be abandoned and ministers might even have to settle for the Alsace-Lorraine of 1870.

These awkward issues have also to be seen in the context of the American intervention in early April. For a time it could appear that the United States and Russia stood together in a war for democracy which could also mean a victory untarnished by the aspirations even of Britain and France. Wilson's decision to advise the Congress that the country should go to war was hardly precipitate. It had cost him much agony to come to the point and perhaps only German insouciance in pursuit of unrestricted submarine warfare gave him his opportunity. Even at the point of intervention, however, he took pains to distance himself from Britain and France. The United States was not their ally, only an associate. The distinction was not of much practical importance and its purpose was symbolic – the United States was different. The air was thick with old notions of the youth, vigour and innocence of the American people. Having finally committed himself to the war – it was only months earlier he had been re-elected as the man who had kept America out of the war – it had to be a struggle to make the world safe for democracy. The United States was not directly threatened, and would not be, and this fact alone gave the American approach to war aims a different colouring. Even if he lacked immediate military strength, Wilson may have calculated that the balance in Europe was such that he would soon be able to exert pressure on Britain and France. Balfour hurried over from London and tried to make a clean breast of the secret treaties. Viviani hurried over from Paris and made a rather less clean breast. Either way, Wilson seemed surprisingly uninterested. A little later, thinking to ingratiate himself, Ribot uttered the sacred words 'League of Nations', only to be told that discussion of the idea was premature. Ribot set up his own commission. The British had the same experience. The restoration of Alsace-Lorraine evoked no enthusiasm across the Atlantic and, even more alarming, now found a similar reception in London. An additional buffer state was thought out of the question. It rather looked as though war aims were out of fashion.

Just at that point, however, the Vatican made its attempt at mediation (see p. 159). The French were hostile, the British luke-warm, but the presbyterian Wilson could hardly wait to reply and did so without consultation in late August. The president explicitly criticized talk of indemnities, the dismemberment of empires and exclusive economic leagues. He contrasted the aspirations of the German people with those of the German autocracy. With 'genuine representatives' of the former, a settlement might be reached. It suddenly seemed possible that even the Kaiser was imposed upon by a small band of military autocrats. Both Britain and France trembled on the brink of negotiations with the enemy, but their interests did not coincide. Some members of the war cabinet, perhaps Lloyd George himself, thought that the Germans might find a formula for Belgium and prod Vienna into finding one for Serbia if, as seemed likely, they could extend their domination over large areas of north-eastern Europe. If the Russians were not going to fight for themselves, why should Britain? The prospect of two great empires emerging from the war, the British and the German, was not entirely displeasing. Over the previous six months, the position of the Habsburg monarchy had frequently been weighed in the balance. The 'oppressed nationalities' developed more extensive organiza-tions and ambitions, with more encouragement from London and Paris. In London, at any rate, though ministerial opinion naturally differed in emphasis, support for their cause was tactical rather than from the heart. Prince Sixte de Bourbon, a sort of Belgian, who hap-pened to have the Austrian emperor as his brother-in-law, produced a letter from him which expressed interest in a negotiated peace, even a separate peace. Lloyd George was exhilarated by the prospect and would happily have forgotten his previous assertions that the Serbs and the Habsburg nationalities almost possessed the virtues of the Welsh. However, at an Allied conference at St Jean de Maurienne in April 1917 Sonnino blocked the scheme on behalf of Italy. Though not often so decisive, that was chiefly the Italian role. The Italian government had come into the war for specific territorial objectives and for no other reason. It would therefore have been galling to have been deprived of them in a settlement which ensured the survival of the Habsburgs. By June, the Sixte initiative was dead, though the British in particular lived in hopes of a comparable approach from Vienna. By early autumn it remained the case that the British cabinet did not feel committed to the Poles and might have acquiesced, in effect, in an Austrian *Mitteleuropa*. For the moment, it was a minority which appeared to take the view that Germany retained strong westward ambitions and which feared that even a whisper of an approach to Berlin might then be communicated to Russia, completely destroying the will to fight and, conceivably, even producing a *bouleversement* of alliances. From his perspective, Lenin interpreted these events as an attempt to make peace at Russia's expense.

The French view was somewhat different. There could scarcely be the same weakening of resolve to gain watertight arrangements for Belgium and Alsace-Lorraine. Likewise, there was no attraction in the British and the German empires being the two to survive the war. There was ample historical precedent for a link with Vienna but the difficulties in achieving that have already been rehearsed. It was only a distant possibility. There remained the problem of the Poles. One solution, which got nowhere, was to 'offer' a reunited Poland to Vienna. Otherwise, it appeared to some members of the French government that the increasing Russian disintegration left no choice but to come out boldly in favour of a united and independent Poland. In September the prime minister went further in this direction than ever before and pressed the British to share his enthusiasm. Such a Poland was no doubt splendid but more sober spirits thought that this goal had been announced at the point when its achievement seemed least likely. The little Polish force on French soil would be lucky if it ever saw Warsaw. An alternative was to grasp the nettle directly and get into some kind of contact with Berlin. Not to be outdone by princes, it happened that the current French war minister, Painlevé had a mistress with Austrian siblings. German agents in Switzerland reported to Berlin that he might be prepared to reach an understanding. Alsace-Lorraine could not be abandoned, but perhaps the Germans might accept commercial and colonial concessions in lieu. Inevitably, it was difficult to know the strength of these feelers and of others in which Belgians were involved. When Painlevé became prime minister in September he seems to have thought that he could get a settlement on Alsace-Lorraine which would be politically tolerable. The opportunity, if it ever existed, disappeared in circumstances of equivocation and misunderstanding which perhaps necessarily hedge around such delicate exchanges. France could not go it alone and by now Lloyd George had sniffed out a 'snare' in the whole business.

Britain and France had to fight on. They were caught. To have reached a settlement at this juncture would perhaps be the last occasion on which they could do so before American views would become of great and perhaps decisive consequence. Even if the prospect of gains elsewhere might make the Germans more accommodating in the West, from a longer-term French perspective that could only confirm German domination over the continent of Europe as a whole. Fighting on might yet make possible greater guarantees in the West and, through German defeat, a counterweight in the East in the shape of Poland. Equally, however, such a con- tinued struggle would take place increasingly under 'Anglo-Saxon' auspices and produce a peace which would be little more congenial. It is not surprising that there was a pervasive pessimism and uncer- tainty at the highest political levels.

In general, throughout the summer, the prospects for the realiza- tion of German war aims looked good. The submarine campaign was going well, though perhaps not well enough. The situation in the East was promising. Nevertheless, internally, as elsewhere, there were those prepared to contemplate what their opponents called a 'peace of renunciation'. However, in May, making what turned out to be his last public speech as chancellor, Bethmann Hollweg appeared still to endorse a programme of war aims which would con- firm German control over territory she presently occupied. Such con- firmation brought fresh difficulties with Vienna. Pessimism was spreading there and Czernin urged that contacts through Prince Sixte should be energetically pursued and, to encourage the chances of success, Germany might show a certain flexibility. Bethmann was sceptical but not altogether intransigent.

In the East, the aspirations of the two powers remained difficult to reconcile. Neither party was content to leave its joint acquisitions to be allocated at the end of the war. The Austrians reluctantly felt that the only way the Germans might be persuaded to make concessions in the West was to renounce their aspirations to Poland and hope to obtain compensation at the expense of Romania. Yet in both capitals divided counsels remained, and neither side revealed the full complexity of each other's thoughts and feelings, though there were frequent meetings to discuss war aims. It distressed Vienna that, notwithstanding the evident scope for Germany in the Baltic, she entertained ambitions in the Balkans. Despite anxious pleas for moderation from Emperor Karl in June, the Germans remained confident and unpersuaded. Vienna had little option but to fall in line. Much would depend on what happened inside Russia. There was a possibility that the Provisional government would come to terms – if Germany scaled down her ambitions. Militarily, however, it did not seem that such a reduction was at present called for. It might be better to do everything possible to promote discord between moderates and extremists, by secret means, and trust that in a matter of months the Russian empire would be incapable of resistance. Hence the willingness, amongst other activities, to facilitate Lenin's return to Petrograd from Switzerland in April. In this pregnant transaction both sides had no illusions about the other but saw the advantages to be gained. The disintegration of Russia would permit a separate peace, the consolidation of objectives in the East and the chance to deliver a final blow in the West, even if disintegration was achieved by the establishment of a revolutionary regime. For Lenin, the commitment to peace offered the path to power in a revolution which would transform Russia and engulf the world. If the German government survived and the revolution succeeded, their enmity might later be intense, but for the moment they needed each other. Time and timing might be of the essence.

In Germany, some of the confidence of late spring and early summer was slipping away. Neither in the West nor the East had military success been achieved; a further winter of campaigning began to look inevitable, and that could only exacerbate the internal strains. Already the pressure for the introduction of the equal franchise in Prussia looked irresistible. After a complicated struggle Bethmann Hollweg was replaced by a nonentity. There was a 'peace resolution' to be debated in the Reichstag, moved by Erzberger, leader of the Catholic Centre party. Passed on 19 July, it claimed that Germany was concerned solely with the integrity of her own territory and sought a peace of understanding. It rejected territorial acquisitions imposed by force. The resolution could be taken to mean that the government would have to take note of a parliamentary majority in favour of a peace more or less based on the status quo. Yet Erzberger made it clear that to reject territorial acquisitions by force did not exclude a host of arrangements in both West and East which would ensure German dominance. It was beneficial to remind Washington that Germany did have a parliament; what its resolution actually meant would clearly depend on circumstances. In fact, when it came to handling the papal intervention over the next few months, the

Reichstag had little influence in the matter. The pope was reminded, amongst other things, that Germany was championing the rights of the Ukraine, Finland, the Baltic provinces, Flanders, Ireland, Egypt and Persia. While that initiative lapsed, in all the manœuvrings that accompanied it the Germans sensed that the British were indeed nibbling at a settlement. They did not want to fight for Alsace-Lorraine and wished to forestall American supremacy. With great difficulty, the basis of what might be an acceptable arrangement over Belgium was drawn up. If it had been put to the test it might not in the end have been politically acceptable within Germany. However, the essential precondition, a specific British undertaking to open peace negotiations, never arrived. Attention in October and November switched back to the intractable issue of Poland and relations with Vienna. The vision of *Mitteleuropa* still beckoned, though its structure and composition fluctuated. And the Bolshevik revolution was imminent.

The events inside Russia in November 1917 had a fundamental effect on the aspirations of all the belligerents. One of the Bolsheviks' first actions was to issue an invitation to all peoples and governments to conclude a general peace without annexations or indemnities and on the basis of full respect for the right of peoples to self-determination. The German government, rather proud of 'its' revolution, accepted with alacrity, anticipating that it would only be the Central Powers who would respond. Hostilities were suspended in early December and an armistice concluded in the middle of the month. The Bolsheviks could not renege on their commitment to peace without forfeiting a major element in their support, yet to acquiesce in a large loss of territory risked inciting a patriotic counter-revolution in circumstances where their control was still far from complete. The Germans did not hesitate. It would no doubt be possible to accommodate their wishes for the Baltic states and Poland within the Bolshevik formula, and steps were taken to establish satisfactory national councils. There was already a democratic republic of the Ukraine to hand and negotiations proceeded to conclude a separate peace with its Rada (Council).

After initial pleasantries, it did not take long for both the Germans and the Bolsheviks to realize that they did not have quite the same understanding of the words 'self-determination'. Even the paraphernalia of open diplomacy and the presence of Trotsky as chief negotiator at Brest-Litovsk in January 1918 could not disguise the weak Bolshevik position. On 18 January a map was presented disclosing starkly the territory Russia would have to lose. Trotsky returned for consultations with the Central Committee, which was split on whether or not to accept the terms. In the end, his policy of 'neither war nor peace' was endorsed; it was hoped world revolution would turn up if there was further delay. On the German side there was concern at the delay and mild consternation at the extent of German aims. The Austrians also wanted a speedy conclusion and pressed for the negotiations with the Ukraine to be separately brought to an end. However, on 9 February Trotsky and the Russian delegation departed from Brest-Litovsk with the extended armistice due to expire a week later. When it did so, the Germans advanced further, consolidating the detachment of the Ukraine from Russia and advancing to give protection along the Baltic littoral. Progress towards Petrograd seemed imminent and on 24 February Lenin persuaded the Central Committee, though not by a large majority, that there was no alternative but to accept the German terms – which had hardened in the interval. The treaty of Brest-Litovsk was signed on 3 March and had been ratified in both countries by the end of the month. There was general satisfaction in Germany at what had been achieved, though some socialists thought that the test of opinion in Estonia, Latvia, Lithuania, Poland and the Ukraine had not been exhaustive. It could be observed that territory once to have been liberated from the sceptre of the tsar had been delivered from the Bolshevik bandits. The principle of national self-determination had been honoured.

Meanwhile, the principal negotiators of the Central Powers were busy in Bucharest settling between themselves, not altogether amicably, the fate of Romania. And, further east, there were seemingly endless possibilities for peeling away Georgia, Armenia and other regions from Russia under suitably protective arrangements. The gallant Turkish ally was urged to desist from Pan-Turanian fantasies. And when all this was finished there was the final shape of *Mitteleuropa* to look forward to, and it was by no means clear that the Bolsheviks could be allowed to survive unmolested. Perhaps Kaiser Wilhelm and Lenin could become friends after all. Meanwhile, however, it was important to turn west and win the war.

In Western Europe and the United States, the Bolshevik revolution was an embarrassment. President Wilson's attitude hardened through the summer of 1917. 'Conquer or submit' he had told the Russian Provisional government and was so unenthusiastic about the proposed Stockholm conference that the State department declined to issue passports to American socialists who wished to attend. He contrasted the German people with their autocratic rulers but it was not pleasant to think of them becoming imbued with revolutionary socialism as a means of ending the war. American progressivism was indubitably best for the world yet Wilson felt that he was now in danger of being outbid by the Bolsheviks. There was no reason why the devil should have all the best tunes, and Wilson answered back with his Fourteen Points on 8 January. He wanted to reassure progressives everywhere, not least in Germany, that the liberal cause was back 'under the patronage of its real friends', as he had put it in declaring war on Austria-Hungary the previous month. Conquest, expansion and secret covenants belonged to days 'gone by'. It was time to formulate a new era, based on open diplomacy, freedom of the seas, freedom of trade, limitation of armaments, self-determination, the end of colonialism and, finally, a general association which would hallow and secure the new order. Powerful speeches and propaganda boosted this enterprise. Only three days earlier, Lloyd George too had felt obliged to make a fresh declaration of war aims. Over the previous few months he had thought it unseemly to air the matter in public, but was now persuaded that both domestic and international opinion required a statement. At the end of November Lord Lansdowne published a letter in the *Daily Telegraph* (he had argued privately on similar lines a year earlier) urging moderate war aims and a willingness to negotiate. The embraces he received for this step were not aristocratic and an incongruous, though ephemeral, 'Lansdowne-Labour' committee emerged to give backing to his views. Henderson uttered comparable sentiments about 'anti-imperialist' war aims. Lloyd George took the view that an Irish marquess could not point the way forward to anything and, after consultations with colleagues, spoke on 5 January.

His remarks on Alsace-Lorraine and territory occupied by the Central Powers followed conventional lines, though the Bolsheviks were warned that if they were so foolish as to conclude a separate peace they would not receive help (Britain did not recognize the regime in Russia). Italy and Romania had legitimate demands for territorial adjustment. The nationalities of Austria-Hungary should have genuine self-government, but that was reconcilable with the existence of the Habsburg monarchy. Non-Turkish elements in the Ottoman empire should have their separate 'national conditions' recognized. The future of German colonies would be settled at a peace conference. 'New diplomacy' rhetoric concluded the speech. He too looked to the 'creation of some international organization'. Given the armistice in the East, he felt it unlikely that the Germans would want to pursue his terms any further. If they had shown any inclination to do so he would probably have responded. That, together with a certain coolness which Lloyd George displayed on Alsace-Lorraine, was the reason why the new French premier, Clemenceau, declined to come to London for discussions in advance of the speech. The French reaction to the gravity of their predicament was a commitment in mid-December to a 'united, independent, indivisible' Poland. Not having many Poles, Lloyd George could not understand this enthusiasm. He wondered, naughtily, whether the United States, which did have Poles, would like to send an army into Central Europe. However, he made a tolerable allusion to Poland in his 5 January speech. Clemenceau was more worried about the 'Anglo-Saxons' and Alsace-Lorraine. He kept emphasizing that the future of the provinces was a moral question, by which he meant it should not be subjected to plebiscites. By dint of a disingenuous acceptance of the Fourteen Points he began to feel that he was getting his way.

Unfortunately for the Allies, there was no guarantee that the war could be won by public declarations. Given the Russian débâcle, it seemed in both London and Paris that only the Habsburg monarchy could act as a counter-weight to German influence. There was information that Vienna was not happy with German activity in the Ukraine. Both Western powers, without disclosing the fact, tried to set up schemes to negotiate a separate settlement, having received the usual tantalizing hints through the usual channels that this might be possible. General Smuts made himself an expert on the monarchy in a short time – but to no avail. The French contacts came out into the open and once more the negotiations collapsed. Emperor Karl had to concentrate on being a faithful ally for a while. France now more or less abandoned the monarchy and cast aside any lingering constraint in the matter of Poland. Its access to the sea was now urged. Through the summer, Czechoslovaks and Yugoslavs were also the beneficiaries of warm sympathy as the notion of a *cordon sanitaire* took hold, at least in embryo. The British, though relieved that there was, *pace*

Shakespeare, no sea coast of Bohemia about which there might be contention, needed to be prodded to give Beneš the recognition and support he needed. It helped that there were 50,000 Czechoslovak troops in Russia who might, apparently, be organized into an effective force to combat the enemy either in the east or west. In the case of the Yugoslavs, reconciliation of their objectives with the commitments to Italy deterred the government from eager recognition.

In all this diplomatic activity there was an element of unreality while the outcome of the war was in the balance. Such uncertainty did not deter Britain and France from attending to that most optimistic of war aims, the League of Nations. The British Phillimore committee reported in March and advocated a series of proposals which stopped far short of the permanent international organization now being pressed by other bodies. The League of Nations had seized the imagination of members of the government, notably of Lord Robert Cecil. They were not going to let the matter rest. Lloyd George liked the League as a peroration rather than a policy and was content to stir the pot. Others suggested the immediate creation of a League of Free Nations which could be joined by others later when they had worked their passage to probity. The French Bourgeois Commission reported on the subject in June and, in disguise, suggested the continuance of the existing alliance against Germany. There was to be the conventional international council, but it also advocated an international army and general staff. Each member would be bound to use its economic, naval and military power to enforce the decisions of the council. Clemenceau could not take the idea seriously and therefore passed the plan on to Washington and London. President Wilson himself could not be persuaded to develop in detail the idea with which he was identified in the public mind. The Germans seemed to have comprehensive plans for everything except the League of Nations.

The war to end war therefore drew to a conclusion with the institutional embodiment of this vision still only in a rudimentary condition. The unexpectedly final months of its course saw the major belligerents still manœuvring by one means or another to safeguard their interests and prepare for the battle of peacemaking that lay ahead. German prospects, which had looked so promising in the spring, were crumbling in the autumn. When the looked-for breakthrough in the West did not materialize and the tide was being reversed, for the first time in the war Berlin tried to take stock and salvage something from the disaster. 'Sacrifices' would be called for in the West. The Belgium that had been hoped for now could not be. The British were to be told that Germany henceforth only had continental aspirations as a land power. The French were to be told that these aspirations lay exclusively in the east. And, of course, there they were not aspirations, they were facts. It was surely not in the interests of the Western world to prise control of vast areas of Eastern Europe away from Germany merely to extend the influence of the Bolsheviks. Such sentiments, naturally refined and elaborated, seemed to offer a way out for those who had guided German policy throughout the war. The man to draw up the contract would be President Wilson; there was ample room for shelter under the capacious umbrella of the Fourteen Points – if a transition to democracy could be arranged to satisfy a former professor of government. The liberal Prince Max of Baden became the new chancellor when Hertling resigned at the end of September. His cabinet, which included Erzberger and Stresemann, seemed genuinely parliamentary in character. Though they sugared the pill by telling the Kaiser that they did not think of giving up the east, Hindenburg and Ludendorff pressed for an armistice and peace as soon as possible. And it was to Wilson that Prince Max addressed notes on 3 October asking him to arrange the conclusion of peace and accepting the Fourteen Points as its basis. Meantime, democratization proceeded apace, instituted from above before existing élites were swept aside. President Wilson would understand the need for that.

Britain and France were alarmed that the war was coming to an end in a way that they had long feared. Skilfully, the Germans were giving President Wilson the chance to shape the settlement that he had been longing for. The French were ever alert and had intercepted Prince Max's first note before Washington conveyed the text to its 'associates'. The contemporaneous capitulation of Bulgaria happened to have brought the British, French and Italian leaders together in Paris. Their minds strayed to this new problem. They agreed that the German approach to Washington had to have a reply. An armistice might well be acceptable, though there was doubt whether a presidential speech was a sufficiently sound basis for its conclusion. It was imperative that Alsace-Lorraine and the left bank of the Rhine be evacuated and it was desirable to occupy the island of Heligoland. Aware that future provision was a diplomatic minefield, matters were more or less left there. The British war cabinet did not

USSR

ESTONIA

LATVIA

LITHUANIA

DENMARK

Danzig

East
Prussia

NETH

GERMANY

POLAND

BELGIUM

Demilitarized
zone

CZECHOSLOVAKIA

Saar

AUSTRIA HUNGARY

ROMANIA

FRANCE

SWITZ

S. Tyrol

YUGOSLAVIA

ITALY

BULGARIA

ALBANIA

GREECE

TURKEY

	German losses
	Bulgarian losses
	Italian gains
••••	Russian empire
——	Habsburg empire
LATVIA	New states

0   200   400 km

0   300 miles

4. Europe after the war

want Washington to feel that it was trying to arrange a peace settlement. It need not have worried. The exchanges with Berlin until 23 October were Wilson's province and he did not wish to upset London and Paris by troubling busy men with information. When he was satisfied, London and Paris were permitted to discuss the specific points in the armistice. Lloyd George expressed certain worries about the freedom of the seas, Clemenceau was still worried about Alsace-Lorraine, but on this high note the war came to an end.

It was only in a superficial sense that Europe was at peace. In the Baltic countries Teutonic knights remained eager to break lances with all comers. The Habsburg monarchy was dissolving. In amazement and joy, mingled with apprehension, the peoples of new states had found freedom. Armenians, who had not found it, felt bitter and betrayed. Jews could look forward to a national home in Palestine, under British tutelage. Arabs could throw off Turkish domination, under British and French protection. Most unexpectedly, the Turks themselves emerged resolute from the Ottoman shell. Japan was moving troops into Siberia. From Murmansk to the Caucasus to Vladivostok the future of 'Russia' was still to be resolved. Just as the Allies had latterly encouraged the ambitions of exiles from the Habsburg monarchy, so the Germans had backed the aspirations of Ukrainian nationalists. The Russian empire might be replaced by many independent states or, on the other hand, Bolshevism might engulf East Central Europe. There was, indeed, much unfinished business in the world and it might prove to be no more stable than it had been in 1914. That would be, in part, for the peace conferences to decide. The intelligence and ingenuity devoted to 'war aims' had in the end been overtaken by the momentum of events. Fundamentally, Grey was right. Diplomats were only the handmaidens of warriors. It was the course of the fighting which shaped the choices they had to make, turned the most ambitious plans to dust and determined the agenda of peacemaking.

5 Home Management

The sombre scale of the war tempts every commentator to ponder over its various phases and compartments. Why did it not end earlier? Why did it end at all? Generals and admirals, private soldiers and able-bodied seamen, politicians and priests, industrialists and trade union leaders – all played their part in winning or losing the war. The 'management' of victory was a test of endurance and ingenuity, calling into play all the administrative skills that early-twentieth-century governments could muster. The orchestration of the war effort was as important as the myriad individual contributions in determining the final outcome. Normally, however, references to national harmony were not to be taken other than metaphorically. No country or army that lost its cohesion could survive and it was upon generals and statesmen that the task of nurturing this unity primarily fell. Such a statement has a deceptive simplicity. It was the nature of war to blur divisions of procedure and practice. It soon became clear that there were few areas of 'normal life' which would remain untouched by its tentacles. The war had to be managed, but the ancient problem of who managed the managers took a new turn.

For some contemporaries in some countries the answer remained simple. War was a matter for generals and admirals. They possessed the lengthy training and professional skill; in short, war was their business. It followed that they should be given as much discretion as possible, both in planning and execution. To subject generals to detailed supervision would only serve to weaken their confidence and capacity. Such an attitude was widespread, at least initially, in most belligerent countries, even those – a minority – where the formal supremacy of civilian government was sturdily established. It was only in 1907, for example, that Italy had its first civilian minister of war, and then for a special reason and briefly. More important than the specific occupant of a ministry of war was how much authority the civilian government had as a whole. It was Clemenceau who, later in the war, summed up the alternative view with his pithy statement that war was too serious a matter to be left to the generals. The special expertise of the military could not be allowed to dictate general policy. It was vital, and for their own good, that soldiers should be subjected to continuous political supervision. It was for politicians to lay down the guidelines and take the broad decisions while leaving to the military a certain freedom, tactically, on the field of battle. It was the task of the military to give the best advice at their disposal, but governments should retain their liberty of judgement. Above all, governments should determine whether to continue to fight or to sue for peace.

Given these contrasting approaches to the central problem of control in war, it is tempting to think of a constant struggle between military and political élites. Indeed, after 1914, soldiers and statesmen everywhere moved into a no man's land of government, groping for an acceptable demarcation of responsibility, never quite sure how far to trust each other. It would be tedious to recount the number of occasions on which mutual irritation and incomprehension found private expression in the view that 'stupid soldiers' or 'bloody politicians' were impeding progress. Yet the antithesis should not be seen as absolute and permanent anywhere – in the last resort they depended upon each other. Arguments about the allocation of resources took place as much within the military machine as between military and civilian departments. More fundamentally, 'soldiers' and 'statesmen' were by no means united among themselves in their interpretation of their roles and functions. Some 'soldiers' were at home in the highest level of government and administration, others found its ways deeply abhorrent. Some 'politicians' relished the opportunity of immersing themselves in the business of war, others could never adapt. Regional or ideological prejudices could cut across and complicate the soldier/statesman distinction. There were particular historical reasons why protestant Irishmen, Pomeranian Junkers and southern Italians, to name but three groups, were disproportionately represented among the officer class of their respective armies and in all of these instances there was scope for political difficulty. In moments of defeat or tension it did not take long for regional animosities to come to the surface. The brittleness of Italian unity, for example, found frequent expression in regional expletives. Giolitti, a Piedmontese, dismissed his rival Salandra as a 'pugliese' (a man from Apulia) and thus self-evidently a liar and a cheat. It was not every English officer who admired a Welsh prime minister (one English-educated Scot in particular did not). In Russia, there was one further variant of this aspect – the employment of non-Russian officers at the highest level, thus helping to prevent the fusion of military and political opposition to the tsar. Stone notes that of 16 men commanding armies when the war began, 7 had German names, 1 a Dutch, 1 a Bulgarian, and of the remainder with Russian names 2 were of Polish descent. All were 'Russian' but some were more Russian than others. Such factors therefore help to explain why civil–military relations were infinitely more subtle than might at first sight appear. Every 'brass-hat' did not have a bone head underneath, and every 'frock' was not a fraud, though to the end the unwritten codes of conduct of the one were mysterious to the other. There was no 'normative' pattern; the state of relations fluctuated with the fortunes of war, the character of individuals, the strength and stability of cabinets and the traditions of each belligerent power.

The British cabinet in 1914 illustrates some of these points. Many of its leading members, not least the prime minister, laid no claim to strategic vision, technical expertise or personal experience of warfare. It was inconceivable that they should hand over responsibility for running the war, but they did feel ill-equipped for the task, with some exceptions. Churchill had been to Sandhurst and had seen little wars around the world. The young Lloyd George had experimented very briefly with soldiering in Caernarfonshire. In consequence, neither lacked confidence in his opinions nor in his right to express them. Initially, though, the cabinet was more concerned to establish national confidence in the military leadership than to worry about its role as the architect of victory. Hence the decision to appoint a non-civilian as secretary of state for war – Field-Marshal Lord Kitchener of Khartoum – and to bring back Fisher as first sea lord. There was also in the background the Curragh 'mutiny', an occasion in June 1914 when certain army officers serving in Ireland did not seem prepared to 'coerce' Ulster into accepting Home Rule at the Liberal government's behest. That incident jolted comfortable notions that the subordination of the British army could be expected in all circumstances. The decision to appoint Kitchener had as a corollary that he was to have very wide authority. His military uniform initially gave him a certain standing amongst his civilian cabinet colleagues. It also seemed to signify that they were not to meddle in his domain. It soon became apparent, however, that the uniform was no guarantee of successful departmental administration. There was, it seems, no necessary correlation between the ability to defeat the Mahdi in the Sudan and the qualities needed to mobilize men and materials for the Great War. He became the target of a press campaign which shouldered him with responsibility for a shell shortage, both in France and the Dardanelles, and therefore supposedly for failure to win the war. Asquith did not feel able to dismiss Kitchener (Fisher, the first sea lord, blew up and resigned) and instead in May 1915 went into coalition with the Conservatives – a step which at least removed the military suspicion that Liberal governments did not know how to conduct wars. Significantly, the new post of minister of munitions was created and Lloyd George, in this office, substantially improved the supplies of shells and guns. He frequently had a shrewder grasp of their requirements than the generals whose views he had to seek.

This was one indication that winning the war might be a matter of industrial organization, and the handling of labour relations, in consequence, of the utmost significance. Yet the evidence suggests that most politicians did not quickly grasp how government itself needed to respond to new priorities. Decision-making in Asquith's initial cabinet was not swift and the efforts to accelerate it proved abortive. After the formation of the Coalition government, Asquith tried ineffectively to run a small war committee alongside the full cabinet. By the end of 1915 Bonar Law was noting that the war could not be brought to a successful issue by the methods currently being pursued. The prime minister made further attempts to form an effective executive body but still too many men wanted to talk about too many things. Weakness in this regard was a major aspect of the dissatisfaction with Asquith which led to his replacement by Lloyd George at the end of 1916. The new prime minister was determined to provide a more effective base for civilian control, establishing a war cabinet of only five members – Bonar Law, Milner, Curzon, Henderson and himself. What mattered to Lloyd George was not a concern for the niceties of party balance, but the formation of an effective personal combination which could take decisions on the pressing issues of the hour, unbothered by humdrum routine matters which could safely be left to others. His innovations in this respect were accompanied by the establishment of his 'garden suburb', a team of specially selected individuals who gave him advice on a host of matters which was distinct from that which he received from the 'proper channels'. This machinery suited him well and the friction with the foreign office or the treasury that sometimes resulted could be regarded as creative.

If he failed to streamline his administration, Asquith did take one important step which had a considerable importance for Britain's overall strategy. Sir William Robertson was brought back from France and made chief of the imperial general staff in December 1915. It was intended that he should be the sole adviser on strategy. At the same time, in France itself, Haig replaced French as commander-in-chief, showing a skill in self-advancement which would have caused any politician to blush. Until the fall of Asquith in December 1916, the Robertson–Haig axis was very strong. Their insistence on the Western front as the significant theatre of operations was unyielding and there was not sufficient will to resist their advice. 'We at the top must stick together and stand firm', Robertson had written to Haig, and he maintained a private correspondence with commanders on all the active fronts. At this stage at least Robertson and other senior commanders tended to have a simple view of Germany. It was a 'decisive' result which he sought, one which could certainly prevent Germany maintaining any naval challenge to Britain, but at the same time he was not interested in ambitious schemes for the political reconstruction of the country or for depriving her of territory either inside or outside Europe. That partly reflected his scepticism in the summer of 1916 about being able to inflict a sufficiently comprehensive defeat to make the exaction of such terms possible, but it also arose from his conviction that a strong Germany was a vital element in the structure of Europe. Robertson did not merely tender advice, he argued his case vigorously in a manner which Lloyd George, Kitchener's successor as war secretary in June 1916, did not find congenial.

When Lloyd George supplanted Asquith in December 1916, Robertson soon felt a new atmosphere and a battle of wits ensued. Significantly, both men had risen from the ranks. Both had shown considerable ruthlessness in dealing with dead-wood politicians and soldiers, but they displayed a strange mixture of confidence and uncertainty in dealing with each other. It is significant that despite his own dabbling in alternative strategies, the prime minister did not feel able, initially, to replace Robertson and instead searched around not very successfully for ways in which his influence and position could be circumvented. After the grim battles from July to November

1917 Lloyd George's impatience with what he saw as the obsession with the Western front again emerged. In September Robertson admitted to Haig that he only stuck to it by instinct and because he could not think of any better strategy with which to replace it. The prime minister argued at the beginning of 1918 that the supreme war council should have an inter-allied reserve. Rightly recognizing that this would mean that Foch would then control overall strategy, Robertson fought a bitter rearguard action against this plan. It seemed that Lloyd George could only get his way by threatening to resign – and he was successful. Robertson was replaced by Sir Henry Wilson, and Haig acquiesced in the new arrangements. Although King George V had lent a sympathetic ear to the pleas of his generals, he knew that he could not risk the constitutional and political catastrophe of a prime ministerial resignation. It was, therefore, to be Lloyd George who 'won' the war. Politicians found Wilson more conciliatory but he, too, fundamentally supported the Western front strategy, though in stating at the close of the war that the main problem was not the Boche but Bolshevism, he was closely attuned to Downing Street. One can therefore assert that, in Britain, civilian control was maintained but, despite some waverings and experiments, it was the strategic view of the military which prevailed. Perhaps Lloyd George was in the final analysis not sufficiently convinced by the views he sometimes advanced, or perhaps he simply could not find soldiers who shared his approach and who were of sufficient standing to replace Robertson or Haig.

In the spring of 1916 Robertson wrote that before the war ended practically anything might happen to 'our boasted British Constitution' and the army was 'the great asset'. After a fashion, however, the constitution displayed considerable resilience. The management of the war, whether by politicians or soldiers, was only possible to the extent that they were sustained by the will to fight on. It was a Liberal government which took Britain to war and which was initially intent on maintaining party government. The Conservatives, however, were equally committed to the war and their only complaint was that it was not being prosecuted with sufficient vigour. The formation of Asquith's coalition in the spring of 1915 brought in leading Conservative figures, but in this administration consciousness of party allegiance still remained strong. Asquith's decision to form this government offended many Liberals, particularly since they retained a majority in the house of commons. Some Conservative backbenchers were not pleased either, seeing their leaders as shoring up a discredited premier, and wanting a purely Conservative government.

Although it was claimed in December 1916 that the Liberal party would come together again when the war emergency was over, Lloyd George's accession to office marked a major shift in political alignment. His position rested upon his own brilliance and dynamism rather than the well-drilled support of a majority party. That gave him a unique freedom of manœuvre and capacity to act as a national leader 'above party', yet also made him vulnerable if things went wrong. The unobtrusive backing of Bonar Law, the Conservative leader, was a necessary adjunct to this style of government. In fact, although Lloyd George did have moments of difficulty, the war did seem to have thrown up a 'national majority' and that coalition won a sweeping electoral victory in December 1918. Although that was on an extended franchise, the verdict could be taken as a kind of retrospective endorsement of the wartime administration – there had been no general election for eight years. Whether Lloyd George had stumbled across the ingredients of a lasting 'National Party' in the form of the fusing together of his wartime Liberal and Conservative support remained to be seen. It was undoubtedly true that the old Liberal party had been dealt blows by the strains of war which fatally destroyed its cohesion. It had to witness interference with its sacred principles of free trade and *laissez-faire* and also to endure the imposition of conscription. The Conservative party had strengthened its position, yet it was saddled with/indebted to a prime minister who might yet destroy its cohesion too.

It was in the Labour movement that potential opposition to the national consensus was located. The decision to go to war had resulted in the emergence of separate 'pro' and 'anti' groupings both in the trade unions and the Labour party, embodied respectively in Arthur Henderson and Ramsay MacDonald. Those who supported the war were firmly in the ascendancy and even MacDonald's 'pacifism' in August 1914 may have been as much tactical as ideological. Certainly he was not a 'non-resister'; he supported 'national defence,' and his criticism of the decision to intervene related more to the prewar conduct of British diplomacy. In this he was joined by a small number of dissident Liberals and radical intellectuals and publicists. The Union of Democratic Control (UDC) which they founded was in theory not against the war as such but concentrated on trying to devise mechanisms which would allow 'the people' more effectively to control the policy made in their name. There was a supposition that 'the people' were more pacific than their governments. Only by the middle of the war, however, and strongly after 1917, did its influence spread and become fused with a wider public consideration of war aims to which the government had to respond in some measure. The UDC and some leading figures in the Independent Labour Party (ILP), where anti-war sentiment was most expressed, were subjected to certain harassment and a degree of surveillance from the police, yet even at the most gloomy moments of the war their opinions were never suppressed. Bertrand Russell, the philosopher, who threw himself wholeheartedly into these activities, did have a short but not too onerous spell in prison. When conscription was introduced in 1916 it had been feared by the government that it would arouse massive resistance, but opposition turned out to be much less than critics had promised. The United Kingdom did at the same time introduce legislation which recognized a 'conscientious objection' to fighting and made possible the provision of alternative service. It did not prove easy to define this category satisfactorily and to determine how far, if at all, it should include objections on political as distinct from religious grounds. Some objected to the alternative service provisions and found themselves in prison. This very small but vocal minority attracted a good deal of attention and some sympathy even from supporters of the war.

War weariness and disillusion with the professed objectives of the fighting certainly spread from 1917 onwards, but in the year that remained it never solidified into a coherent and united body of opinion capable of so undermining support for the war that the government could not carry on. Particularly after Henderson's resignation from the war cabinet in August 1917, differences of opinion in the Labour movement became less important. The emphasis was placed on a future 'just peace' which it believed to be available sooner than the government seemed to think. Events in Russia, too, caused a good deal of interest and excitement in certain quarters. A convention had been held in Leeds in June to celebrate the overthrow of the tsar and plan a network of soviets throughout Britain. Such activities caused some anxiety in government circles, and they were closely monitored. There was a new mood, too, in industry and a rash of strikes and disputes caused the appointment of a special commission of enquiry. Investigating conditions in different industrial regions, it reported that the rapid rise in the cost of living lay behind much of this unrest, accompanied in some instances by a deeper-seated sense of antagonism between capital and labour. It was noted that a shortage of beer caused some who might have been otherwise engaged on Saturday evenings to listen to pacifist orators instead. The government responded by introducing additional bonus payments and shelving plans for further dilution of labour. There were disputes in 1918 caused by further government measures to improve recruitment to the army, and a series of strikes on the railways, but leaders of the ILP were adamantly opposed to any attempted political use of industrial strength. If the war produced increasing political strains, it did not shatter the national consensus or more than marginally hinder the willingness to struggle on to victory.

And the empire held firm too, though not without stress and incident. Gandhi, back in India since 1915, confessed in April 1918 that he felt ashamed that 'as a responsible citizen of the empire' he had not been taking his share in the war. He had no 'war record' in the conventional sense of the term. Overcome with remorse, he chose the summer to embark on a recruiting campaign. Other contemporary Indian political leaders were bemused by this activity and could only put it down to the 'queer food' – only fruit and nuts – that Gandhi consumed. In 1916 the Muslim League and the Congress had agreed on a scheme of constitutional reform that would represent a definite step towards self-government – though that unity of objective was somewhat precarious. In August 1917 Montagu, then secretary of state for India, announced in the commons that the government was committed to the increasing association of Indians in every branch of administration. There were to be changes which would move India in the direction of responsible self-government as an integral part of the British empire. It was not clear precisely what this declaration signified, but both 'extremists' and 'moderates' in India confidently expected speedy progress. Yet religious and linguistic tension remained high and could not readily be subordinated in common opposition to the Raj. Pan-Islam was perhaps perceived as the most dangerous threat by the government of India and two prominent journalists, Mahomed and Shaukat Ali, were placed under house arrest. When the extraordinary Annie Besant turned to advocating violence during her Home Rule campaign, she was interned in 1917. None of these figures, however, was 'representative' of what the mass of the Indian population felt either about the Raj or the war. As

Gandhi enrolled his hundredth recruit, it remained to be seen whether the British would reciprocate by deciding that India was indeed worthy of *swaraj*, or self-government.

All the dominions were caught up in unexpected issues as a result of their participation in the war. In all of them, those eager to fight had done so early on, with the result that recruitment had fallen away sharply by 1916. The British government remained eager for dominion manpower, and dominion politicians were anxious not to forfeit the new standing which participation in the war had brought. William Hughes of Australia, prime minister since October 1915, returned from London with a proposal to extend compulsory service to include overseas duty. Put to a national referendum, the proposal was narrowly rejected and caused political turmoil. Hughes left the Labour party and headed a National Coalition dependent upon his erstwhile opponents for support. It was a particular habit among Welshmen at this time. Gaining a strong majority in an election in 1917, and faced by still falling recruitment, Hughes again appealed for extended compulsory service and again failed. He had to make do with a voluntary campaign for the rest of the war. Opposition in 1916 had come from Irish Catholics, led by the archbishop of Melbourne and from some socialists. These objections to an 'English' and 'imperialist' war were strengthened by events in Russia in 1917. If the war had gone on any longer, Australian support might have weakened, but at its close, Hughes's determination to 'speak for Australia' continued to ensure majority backing for the war. That support was even more solid in the case of New Zealand. Society was not divided by the issue of conscription for service overseas. In South Africa, the tensions generated by the initial abortive Afrikaner rebellion did not disappear. In wartime elections, the Nationalists made gains, but the government held on; it even survived their opposing, in parliament in 1918, a motion that God would grant Britain victory. Canadian politics continued to show a divided response to the demands of the war between the two language groups. By 1917, the initial urge to unity could not be sustained. The issue of conscription caused acute disagreement, linked as it was with complaints by *canadiens* about their treatment in their country's armed forces. As in Australia, the party system of 1914 did not survive intact. The divisions inside Canada did not prevent a substantial contribution being made to the war effort, but certainly prevented the full use of the country's manpower. The most difficult problem, from the standpoint of the British government, turned out to be close at hand. The 1916 Easter Rising in Dublin, its suppression and the subsequent treatment of its leaders, was an acutely embarrassing matter, not least in dealings with the United States. The condition of Ireland had the semblance, as the war drew to a close, of an occupied country. It was in the end decided that it was neither possible nor desirable to attempt to impose conscription on Ireland. Thus, although the rebellion had been contained, there was now a marked divergence in political attitudes between Dublin and London, though Irish units in the British army fought on with scarcely a doubt about their loyalty.

It was the case, however, that after Lloyd George became prime minister the war cabinet was occasionally enlarged and formed the imperial war cabinet, which included the dominion leaders. Men such as Borden of Canada and Smuts of South Africa came to London for long periods and from time to time played an important role in decision-making. It was difficult for them to play this role at the centre without losing touch with their domestic publics, but they were able to secure the resolution of the 1917 imperial war conference which stated that the Dominions were 'autonomous nations of an Imperial Commonwealth' and thus to hint that a combined war effort entailed consultation – even if it proved in practice to be on a rather smaller scale than they had anticipated or desired. Taken in the round, however, the 'management' of Britain and the British empire appeared to be one of the major achievements of the war.

Imperial/national cohesion was sustained, and the enemy discomfited, by the use of emergency legislation and propaganda. The Defence of the Realm Act gave the British government extensive powers to restrict activity which might be considered prejudicial to national security. The Defence of India Act came into a comparable category, as did the Australian War Precautions Act. The National Council for Civil Liberties was one body formed in the United Kingdom to express dismay at the powers possessed by government to restrict what it considered to be the legitimate expression of opinion. On the other hand, the press did not find it difficult to conjure up an image of the 'Evil Hun' and the atrocities which he perpetrated. The most popular contemporary novelists put their services at the disposal of the state. It was the historian G. W. Prothero who was the inspiration behind the Central Council for National Patriotic Organizations. A secret war propaganda bureau operated from Wellington House with a special mission to enlighten the United States. It was directed by C. F. G. Masterman, a Liberal politician who could not win elections but might yet win the war. John Buchan guided the Department of Information formed in 1917, Lord Beaverbrook a Ministry of Information in 1918, and Lord Northcliffe was also brought in, using his formidable knowledge of the press and publicity to undermine the enemy's will to fight. Propaganda, Hitler later professed to believe, was a weapon of first importance in England – at least as compared with German efforts. It is difficult, however, to decide whether propaganda was really of such significance. The press scarcely needed to create a patriotic public and there is always a tendency for those whose business is words to believe that words matter supremely. The German nation was scarcely likely to be seduced from its convictions by the odd British balloon, packed with seditious suggestions, which may have crossed the frontier – if the wind happened to be especially favourable.

The management of American intervention was even more a matter of words. During over two and a half years of neutrality, the American people had grown accustomed to a distant conflict which had scarcely been given immediacy even by the German submarine campaign. There was a good deal of less than quiet satisfaction at the internecine activities of the Europeans. It looked as if the twentieth century would be the century of American commerce. Business boomed and was in no mood to let intervention interfere with the advantages which had accrued from the preoccupation of Europeans with killing each other. Intellectuals had argued about the issues at stake since the beginning of the war but, since the 'peace mandate' at the election of November 1916, most Americans had continued to see in these exchanges nothing more serious than academic debate. Progressive reformers, anxious about city slums and corporate power, could not conceive that war would be a necessary and liberating experience. The only conceivable path Wilson could follow was to seek to channel the idealism of the Progressive era into the war itself. In the battle for the American mind, rhetoric became of supreme importance. It was fortunate that intervention coincided with 'the new democracy' in Russia and enabled Walter Lippmann and other writers of like mind to envisage 'a great end' and 'a great hope' – the Federation of the World, no less. It suddenly became apparent that fighting was not entirely alien to American life. Indeed, some young Americans had long since contrived to fight and die in Europe. There was also the celebrated Lafayette Escadrille, privately financed by Americans to allow young men from the United States to fly in the service of France. American field ambulance units had received a good deal of publicity, enabling Ernest Hemingway, John Dos Passos, Malcolm Cowley and others to see the war at first hand. Yet, speaking generally, resigned acceptance rather than exuberant enthusiasm characterized American attitudes. It could scarcely be otherwise when the surprise and fear that had detonated the European consciousness in 1914 were absent. In areas with a strong Irish, German or Scandinavian ethos there was not even that fundamental acceptance. Now that the country was at war, however, the government could not countenance the notion of hyphenated loyalty. To fight in Europe therefore became a test of the solidity of American identity.

American historians speedily devoted themselves to explaining why the country was involved and to devising 'war issues courses' which left no doubt that the struggle was between democracy and autocracy. It was clear, however, that propaganda was too serious a business to be left to the historians. Staffed with muckrakers exuding faith in progress, Wilson established the Committee on Public Information under George Creel. Relying on nothing more than facts, it claimed by the end of the war to have distributed 75 million pamphlets and issued 6,000 press releases. Some 75,000 orators were skilled in getting at the essence of the matter in four minutes. *The Sword of America*, by William Chauncy Langdon, performed in 1917 by the Illinois Drama Federation, is but one example of a patriotic presentation. Persuasion, however, was accompanied by restraint and coercion. At the highest levels, the Espionage Act was vigorously enforced. The postmaster general took particular pleasure in administering the censorship laws and he was given extended powers under the Trading-with-the-Enemy Act. Socialist opponents of the war, who were not negligible in eastern cities, were harassed. It also become apparent that the most lofty aspirations were accompanied, at the popular level, by vendettas and lynchings perpetrated against those whose patriotism seemed at all suspect. Given the plural nature of American society, attempts to identify 'enemy aliens' offered a ready excuse for the settlement of old animosities. Wilson himself professed a willingness to allow opponents of war to 'strut their uneasy hour and be forgotten', confident in the 'calm, indomitable

Power of the nation' – a nation which was boldly rechristening sauerkraut as the liberty cabbage – but the reality was a good deal more murky.

Fighting a war across the Atlantic raised other serious problems of management and control. Preparation for war in Europe clashed with the president's initial intention to be impartial in thought as well as in action. Army leaders had to console themselves with the possibility of intervention in Mexico. The prevailing assumption, even after the declaration of war, was that the American contribution would be mainly naval and financial. However, during May, the secretary of war, Newton Baker, selected General Pershing to command the expeditionary force. He speedily disappeared to London, armed with more freedom to plan than any other commander. Over the months that followed, his major preoccupation was not the government in Washington but those in London and Paris. European politicians in turn found it extraordinary that a general should have such freedom in matters of strategy as Pershing evidently possessed. The American war effort in Europe did indeed seem to be run by military men. It was an extraordinary transformation of their influence within such a short period, to be explained in part by logistical and geographical considerations but also by the commander-in-chief's profound lack of interest in the army which, as president, he required to bring him victory. The inconvenient end of the war prevented Pershing from becoming an even more formidable politico-military figure than he did become. It was indeed a 'short war' for the United States as a whole and neither the American public nor army went through the same cycle of moods as those of the European belligerents. The peculiar people had an appropriately peculiar war.

For both the United Kingdom and the United States the war was inevitably distant from the domestic populations in so far as it was taking place abroad. No such luxury was afforded the continental belligerents. War on the doorstep gave an unwelcome immediacy to problems of management and control. In France at the close of the war political leadership appeared firmly in the ascendancy. Clemenceau formed his ministry in November 1917 and thereafter few doubted that 'the Tiger' was in charge. Before him, there had been four premiers – Viviani, Briand, Ribot and Painlevé. They had been sustained in parliament by the 'union sacrée' of August 1914 when deputies from all parties had been prepared to put their faith in the government of the day and in Joffre. Parliament itself ceased to meet. Even when its sittings resumed, information was passed between leading figures rather than across the chamber. Governments could rely on support, even from unexpected quarters. The Right found the way in which government conducted business quite congenial and was not interested in cries for greater parliamentary control. It was only Painlevé's government of 1917 that was actually defeated in the chamber. Joffre was given very considerable latitude in the first year of the war and he took rather more. It was no secret that parliamentarians were unwelcome at the front – though, since a good many also wore uniforms, ignorance was not as complete as it might otherwise have been. In 1916 the commander-in-chief and the minister of war attracted increasing criticism, especially from Clemenceau. The phrase 'This is in the domain of the high command' made him wild, but his voice, when the censor allowed it full journalistic expression, seemed to be that of one crying in the wilderness. His speech at the secret session discussion of Verdun seems to have been a failure. By the end of 1916, however, the rising total of French casualties caused increasing parliamentary unease. Briand finally brought himself to sack Joffre – though he himself then resigned in March 1917. It was left to Ribot and then Painlevé, in swift succession, to deal with the failure of Nivelle's offensive and the loss of nerve by French troops. Pétain restored discipline, but the politicians were in an increasingly volatile mood. It was expecting too much for the intrigues and hatreds of prewar politics to be submerged for ever. In the summer of 1917 a former premier, Caillaux, and the minister of the interior, Malvy, were arraigned on charges of treasonous contacts with the enemy – a spectacle not available in any other Allied country. Such an event pointed up the loss of morale in French society as a whole, faced by heavy losses and the apparent impossibility of inflicting a defeat on Germany. Perhaps it was best to seek a negotiated compromise? Rumours to this effect, coupled with increasing labour unrest, seemed to suggest that the management of victory was impossible.

Clemenceau had played a key part in obtaining Malvy's resignation. His aged star was in the ascendancy. President Poincaré had little alternative but to ask him to form a government in November 1917. Since the events of that year had led to the abandonment of the 'union sacrée' and socialist opposition was openly declared, few gave the new ministry a long life. However, from the outset, Clemenceau gave evidence of his firm determination to revive the will to fight. He struck out against defeatism, whether on the Right or the Left, and dealt directly with trade union leaders with a mixture of coercion and improved conditions. The bills would have to be paid later, but it was important to win the war beyond everything. Clemenceau's position waxed steadily stronger and was never seriously in jeopardy in the chamber. Not that it was a premiership based upon the artful conciliation of party factions and personalities in traditional fashion. In effect, parliament was bypassed and he succeeded, mysteriously, in speaking to the country and for the country. Parliamentary critics sensed their impotence. An insurrectionary general strike in the Loire in May 1918 was the climax rather than the start of a fresh round of industrial disturbances. Clemenceau's position in France was thus as unusual as Lloyd George's in Britain. His brusque authoritativeness (he was his own war minister and his foreign minister was exceptionally deferential) made it easy, if inaccurate, to describe him as a dictator. His assertion of civilian control, however, did not entail the imposition of an alternative strategy from that advocated by the military. It was rather a question of willpower. Clemenceau's position was also made easier by the fact that when he came into office Foch (chief-of-staff) and Pétain (commander-in-chief) did not form the same kind of partnership in relation to him as Robertson and Haig did in relation to Lloyd George. Bitter disputes lay ahead at the peace settlement but, given the immediate prewar atmosphere of distrust between republican politicians and important elements in the army, and the Dreyfus affair itself, a surprisingly effective partnership between army and government had been forged in France. It was victory of a kind for democracy, though perhaps not for the French chamber. It had required a judicious stiffening of editorial backs and a lubrication of proprietorial purses. It had called for a certain contempt for civil liberty and a willingness to hound political opponents who dared to believe that the independence and honour of France could be subjected to cost-benefit analysis. Clemenceau was prepared to do whatever was necessary to keep France afloat. When the war was over, however, he did not think it necessary to accept the cardinal archbishop of Paris's invitation to attend a *Te Deum* in Notre Dame. He also advised the president of the Republic that his attendance would be inappropriate. Poincaré thought this rather harsh and sent his wife. It was by such acts that the brittle cohesion of France was sustained.

Since the Italian decision to intervene was internally divisive from the outset, it is not surprising that the management of the Italian war effort proved particularly controversial. The debate in the spring of 1915 had, however, not been between 'politicians' and the 'military', but, rather, reflected a deep rift among the political classes. What was the 'will of the people' was uncertain at the time and has remained so. Intervention did mean that the role of the king and parliament became extremely contentious and never ceased to be so. The sequence of events brought little consolation either to extreme Right or Left. The government itself was specially vulnerable in so far as the motivation for participation was avowedly territorial. The achievement of such aims would depend upon the army. Yet the army commander, Cadorna, made it plain that it was not appropriate for the cabinet to know of his military plans. The friction this attitude engendered almost came to a head in the summer of 1916 but Salandra, the prime minister, could not brace himself to dismiss Cadorna. In early June, however, the Liberal government was itself defeated and a new ministry 'of concord, for war and for victory' was formed with a broader political base. Cadorna battled on with scant success while ministerial supporters were locked in the intricacies of ambitious schemes of annexation. By the spring of 1917 the lack of correspondence between the reality and the dream slowly impinged, aided by steadily increasing domestic unrest, particularly in the northern cities. The whiff of revolution could be detected in the events in Turin in August 1917 when 'tanks' had to be used to restore order. Other Italians were impressed by the pope's appeal, in the same month, for peace. A small army mutiny was suppressed by force and Cadorna blamed parliamentarians for the defeatism which he detected everywhere. It could not be denied that the government was inefficient, but its supporters argued that the rifts in Italian politics and society made any firmer direction impossible. Opponents argued that civil anarchy gave the army an impossible task. In late October, Prime Minister Boselli was defeated by a large majority and resigned; within hours, the gravity of the Austrian advance became apparent. It was quite impossible to conceal the extent of the army's disintegration and Cadorna himself issued a communiqué which spoke of the ignominious surrender of some units to the enemy. In these desperate straits, Orlando formed a new government, seeking to establish acceptance in both neutralist and interventionist sections and forming a cabinet accordingly. Cadorna was sacked, not only because of Caporetto, but because his view of the nature of high command made the effective assertion of ministerial authority impossible. General Diaz did indeed prove more co-operative and the government itself survived until the close of the war. Yet parliamentary direction was still fragile, even though the extent of the near-disaster did, for a time, lead to greater national cohesion. The tensions of 1915 had not gone away and were now exacerbated by fresh allegations of mismanagement and inefficiency. Italy's presence among the victorious states offered little comfort when it was apparent that it had not, in the event, played the major part some had anticipated in making possible the war gains which were still sought.

In the three continental empires – Germany, Austria-Hungary and Russia – the management of the war proved an even more difficult and, in the end, impossible task. The issue of authority was never far from the surface. All three empires did now possess parliaments but in no case was the government chosen by or responsible to these bodies, though their assent to particular pieces of legislation was sometimes required. The direction of the war therefore rested with the crown and the ministers it appointed and this fact inevitably complicated the relationships between soldiers and politicians.

In Russia, the tsar appointed his own uncle, Grand Duke Nicholas, as commander-in-chief on the outbreak of war rather than the controversial war minister Sukhomlinov. By 1915, however, the reticence of Duma politicians was being cured. Military failure and evident mismanagement gave them the opportunity to emerge from patriotic silence and demand, at the least, cabinet government and some voice in running the war. For a time, industrialists lent their support to these criticisms. So did elements in the Stavka – the notional supreme command of the army. Dislike of Sukhomlinov was a common feature, but the alliance was tenuous and uncertain of the lengths to which it should take criticism – particularly after the tsar replaced his uncle and took personal command of the army (August 1915). Personnel changes accompanying this move for a time had a beneficial effect upon civil–military relations, but by the end of 1916 criticism was again mounting in the Duma. Influential voluntary organizations which had stimulated the provision of equipment for the army added their voices to the call for a 'government of popular confidence'. Even so, it was possible to see in these exchanges little that endangered the monarchy. While there were republicans, it was the government rather than the tsar himself which was the butt of criticism. At a different level, however, the stresses that the war-effort entailed were becoming ever more apparent. The expansion of industry brought many peasants flooding into cities where they were badly housed, paid and fed – Petrograd was like Turin in this respect. The winter of 1916/17 brought their discontent to a head. By 25 February there was virtually a general strike in the capital but, after an incident in which troops did fire on crowds, about a third of the garrison mutinied. Troops sent by the tsar – who was out of the capital – to suppress the disorders themselves went over to the revolutionaries. The tsar abdicated, but on 3 March Grand Duke Michael refused to pick up the crown.

Then began the confused period during which a Provisional government existed alongside the Petrograd Soviet of Workers' and Soldiers' Deputies. Everything – except the presence of the German army at the gates – was temporary. In these circumstances it is a little difficult to speak of the management of the war when the two most important bodies in the country disagreed about the necessity for its prosecution. Added to which, in the new circumstances, the position and role of the commander-in-chief was a constitutional conundrum. Kornilov, who took this post in late July, had little doubt after the failures of the early summer that only a vigorous reassertion of discipline at the front and at home (that is to say, against the Bolsheviks who were steadily gaining strength in trade unions and the soviets) could prevent disintegration. In late August, there was a clash between Kornilov and Kerensky, now the prime minister in the Provisional government. Whether there was a 'counter-revolution' in mind, and what that phrase means, is still a tangled and complicated question. No attack on Petrograd in fact took place, but the mutual accusations of treachery that followed in the wake of this extraordinary affair contributed to the undermining both of the army and the notional Provisional government. Hitherto, the Bolsheviks had been opposed to an insurrection, but Lenin judged that the moment was ripe and was vindicated by his subsequent success. The irony was that, by this stage, Kerensky had made himself commander-in-chief but the process by which he had achieved it meant that he could neither manage the war nor his own political survival.

In Austria-Hungary, the marginal contribution which it was anticipated that the imperial parliament (Reichsrat) would make to running the war was expressed by turning its premises into a military hospital. Quite properly, the government went about its business according to the powers open to it under the constitution without the benefit of this distraction. There was little doubt that a meeting of the Reichsrat would only see the reappearance of nationality politics. However, the parliaments of Hungary and Croatia did meet and could offer comment on the conduct of the war, in so far as it concerned them. The non-unitary structure of the state makes it difficult to generalize about the means whereby the war was waged. It proved impossible for legal and administrative reasons to co-ordinate the activity of the monarchy as a whole. Substantial areas were designated as operational zones and subjected to military control. It was a military office, for example, which arrested Kramář, the leader of one section of Czech political opinion. It was the absolutism which led Friedrich Adler, a German-Jewish socialist, son of one of the best-known European socialists, Viktor Adler, to precipitate a change of minister-president by shooting the existing holder of the post in October 1916. Before his death in the following month, the emperor found a replacement but felt no urge to recall the Reichsrat. The young Karl, his successor, moved swiftly at the end of the year: he found a new minister-president, foreign minister, and chief of the general staff and made himself supreme head of the monarchy's armed forces. Preparations went ahead for the assembling of the Reichsrat at the end of May 1917. The leaders of the various national 'parliamentary clubs' denounced the dual system of the monarchy and talked about autonomy under the House of Habsburg. In June, Karl was forced to turn to a civil servant for a replacement minister-president and he (Seidler) did succeed in forming a cabinet drawn from the major national groupings. However, by the winter of 1917/18, strikes and industrial unrest on a considerable scale indicated that the empire was confronted by social divisions as well as nationality problems. Returning prisoners of war further complicated matters. 'Solution' followed 'solution' in rapid succession and another civil servant became minister-president – all to no avail. Before his own downfall, Czernin wrote feelingly to his emperor of the difficulties in waging war in a country only united through the dynasty as compared with one where the people shared national ideals. The management of Austria-Hungary's war proved beyond the capacity of even a vigorous young emperor and his bureaucratic/political advisers.

Germany, too, was a puzzling mixture of autocracy and constitutional monarchy, further complicated by 'federal' and 'imperial' elements. Administrative decentralization jostled uneasily with strong centripetal forces. The states possessed real powers, with Prussia the most conspicuous among them. It was by virtue of his position as king of Prussia that the emperor derived his power, and the chancellor likewise as minister-president of Prussia. The Reichstag, elected by universal male suffrage since 1912, could vote down legislation but could not impose its wishes on the Prussian Landtag (elected by a three-tier voting system which ensured conservative preponderance), the Bundesrat or the chancellor. There was an anti-government majority in the Reichstag but no consensus among socialists, Catholics and liberals. The government of Germany, in peacetime, in these circumstances was a very complicated business when the pressures exerted by various industrial and agrarian groups are also taken into account. At first, the war seemed to simplify the task. In the fashionable sociological language of the day, there appeared to be a real chance that this energetic but ramshackle *Gesellschaft* (society) would be transformed into a *Gemeinschaft* (community). The Social Democrats voted for war credits (though differences existed among them) and the Kaiser declared that he no longer recognized classes or parties. This was *Burgfrieden* or 'truce of the fortress'. Even that phrase indicates that the army was to be allocated a major domestic role. Three blasts of the trumpet gave deputy commanding generals under the Prussian Law of Siege the obligation to maintain 'public safety' – a term capable of generous interpretation.

Initially, the government had hoped that it would not need to translate its assurances of good will into specific measures until after the war ended. By 1916, however, it was forced to make some concessions in trade union law and the Kaiser had made a somewhat equivocal declaration which was taken to be a reference to the Prussian voting system. By this date, too, the crisis in the management of the war was increasingly apparent. As chancellor, Bethmann Hollweg saw the need for internal reforms and began to lose confidence in the possibility of total victory, but by the same token his own position was by no means secure. The first struggle concerned Falkenhayn's position as chief of staff. After his failure at Verdun and in the context of setbacks also in the east and south-east, pressure for his removal mounted. Odd bedfellows conspired to this end, but the struggle was fierce. Falkenhayn's contempt for politicians was reciprocated – the chancellor resented his attempted interference in political matters – but the Kaiser stood by him. Eventually, however, after a bout of tears, the Kaiser agreed to his replacement by Hindenburg with Ludendorff at his side. Hindenburg's great blue eyes inspired a remarkable number of people with confidence which he could not hope to satisfy. Mysteriously contriving to ignore Ludendorff's ruthless ambition, Bethmann

Hollweg professed satisfaction with the elevation of the popular hero.

It soon became clear that, under the new leadership, the high command in the *Grosse Hauptquartier* gave itself a mission from the German people in the fields of economic and foreign policy which did not depend upon the approval of the chancellor. Such new dynamism inevitably entailed a mass of overlapping and competing bureaucracies in the name of efficiency. The 'Hindenburg programme' was designed to maximize German productive capacity and such measures as the Auxiliary Labour Law of December 1916 were designed by the High Command and merely passed by the Reichstag. The military mind was no more enamoured of irreverent capitalism than it was of anarchic socialism and it is not easy to categorize the army-inspired interventions in 'conservative' or 'radical' terms. There were even suggestions that Hindenburg should formally become a kind of military dictator, but he rejected the idea. It was better to operate behind the scenes.

The most notable casualty was the chancellor, Bethmann Hollweg, in July 1917. He sensed that Germany's internal situation was deteriorating and was convinced that the promise of universal suffrage and its implementation in Prussia was imperative. But he had alienated the Catholic leader, Erzberger, and lost a majority in the Reichstag. The Kaiser was warned that Hindenburg and Ludendorff would resign if the chancellor was not dismissed. Bethmann Hollweg removed the necessity for this step by resigning. The power of the High Command was demonstrated and the Reichstag's peace resolution nullified. Michaelis, the new chancellor, was a senior Prussian civil servant and the High Command left him in no doubt that it did not want a repetition of his predecessor's weakness. Michaelis only lasted a few months, though it was not military meddling which brought him down but rather an invigorated Reichstag, which the army had itself desired when Bethmann Hollweg was the target, but which it now had misgivings about. Hertling, the new appointment, was not the army's candidate, but his scope for manœuvre was limited. It remained the High Command which decided when the 'military situation' would permit suffrage reform. It remained the High Command which played a major part in determining 'foreign policy' in the East. Yet while it appears that in the final years of the war its management was fundamentally in the hands of the generals, that was neither absolutely nor unequivocally the case. Forms, at least, were still frequently observed and setbacks were experienced in the complex interplay of decision-making. And in the end the army did not win the war, with all that inevitably stemmed from this failure.

In the last resort, there remained the Kaiser himself, the Supreme Warlord, the ineffective arbiter between competing interests and aspirations. For the most part encamped in the *Grosse Hauptquartier*, he nevertheless failed to exercise that authority which he possessed. In a system which depended upon a monarch to carry out this integrating function there could be no more fatal flaw. Indeed, upon the king, one is tempted to say, depended the successful management of war in the circumstances of Europe in 1914–18; upon the man, not upon the office. It was not a good war for monarchs. For one reason or another, Wilhelm, Nicholas, Franz Josef, Karl all lacked the capacity or the will which it was vital that they should display. The Allies were better served. Although his government took up residence at Le Havre, King Albert stayed on Belgian territory with his army and refused to leave it. King Victor Emmanuel seems to have been the only Italian, in the wake of Caporetto, who believed that his army could stay in the war and successfully persuaded Lloyd George, in eloquent English, that this was the case. King George V angrily denied that he was German and changed his family name from Saxe-Coburg-Gotha to Windsor to make his position quite clear. And, in distant Glasgow, even President Poincaré was thought by the students of its ancient university to be sufficiently charismatic to warrant election as their Rector. Amidst the play of profound forces and great armies, the role of the head of state, for good or ill, is not to be overlooked.

6 The Experience of War

No man who took part in the First World War ever completely shook off the experience. Individuals struggled to come to terms with what they had seen and heard. For some, the only solution was silence. There was no way in which it was possible to communicate with those who had not been through it themselves. The inadequacy of language itself was exposed. Words gained fresh meaning in the context of war and vocabularies became hopelessly confused. Fathers who had every conventional reason for pride in their part in the conflict chose not to tell their children what they did in the war. The gap in experience could not be bridged by trite phrases or plain narrative. It was better to forget and resume ordinary life as though nothing had happened. For many that was never possible. Ivor Gurney, English poet and composer, died in a mental hospital in 1937, twenty years after he had been gassed in France. He had gone on writing, convinced that the war had not come to an end. Other men who appeared to retain their poise and composure were secretly scarred. Many years later they would wake up in the night, still unable to shake off some lingering horror. In general terms, it took many writers a decade before they were ready with an appropriate novel or memoir. And at that distance experience may be refined and embroidered so as to render it no longer authentic.

Even to use such a word, however, is to beg the question. There was no single war shared by all who took part in it. Each battle triggered off complex emotions. Fears mingled with exhilaration, disgust with exultation. Some men who had never killed before killed without remorse. Others, when the moment had passed, were sick. There is a natural tendency to peer back at the war through slits in trenches at desolate mud, to see a rat in every corner, to think of men freezing to death on the Eastern front. That is indeed one savage image of war. Yet it is mistaken to see in the conditions of battle something totally alien to the experience of most soldiers. To move from a Glasgow or Vienna tenement, from a coalmine in the Rhondda or the Ruhr, to the battle front could even seem an improvement in living conditions. Food was frequently better. There was more exercise and even more 'fresh air'. In no army did those who survived fight all day and every day from 1914 to 1918. There were regular periods away from the front line. There were visits home – though these could prove as disturbing as they were relaxing. War was often dull and boring, with nothing very much happening. Not every regiment showed the same foresight as some British cavalry regiments in bringing over packs of hounds for the duration. There was always football. There were concerts. There was laughter. There was even Harry Lauder walking about in an unmilitary kilt specially designed to confuse French villagers. Yet there was an inescapable underlying intensity which not even a jocular Jock could dissipate. Lauder recounts that up near the front line he was suddenly possessed by a savage desire to rush at the guns ahead and turn them to his own 'mad purpose of vengeance'. The Huns had killed his beloved son. They had also killed Mr Asquith's son Raymond. The same story could be repeated on the other side. The 'generation of 1914' became 'the lost generation'.

In these circumstances the maintenance of morale was crucial. If the troops would not fight the war could not go on. In the early years it seemed, straightforwardly, that there was a job to be done and it had to be done as efficiently as possible. They might not enjoy the war, but the most unexpected people seemed to be resilient under fire, unsettling the status hierarchies of peacetime. When they became non-commissioned officers, the practical common sense of shop assistants or factory foremen frequently became of supreme importance. Men soon came to appreciate which officers they could trust. Officers soon came to understand what their men could or could not do. It was a working relationship the effectiveness of which did not conform to any easy pattern. Authority rested upon an integrity of personal behaviour which transcended class, language or accent. One study of the 2nd Scottish Rifles at the battle of Neuve Chapelle in 1915 concludes that at this level the morale of an army depended upon such factors. In every European army there was an element of give and take, rather than a merging of social identities. One study of the French army concludes that officers frequently established an arrangement by which, in return for obedience in battle, there was minimal interference with the men otherwise. British private soldiers were frequently surprised by the sloppiness in appearance and dress of their French counterparts. During the battle of the Marne the French historian Marc Bloch noted in his fellow soldiers a kind of grave contentment, if only that they were all still alive. Death, he later felt, only appeared terrible when it came close. Men dreaded coming under fire, or returning to it, but once there they ceased to tremble. It was clear to him, however, that few soldiers thought of their country when conducting themselves bravely. What guided them was a sense of personal honour, reinforced by group loyalty. Peasants – and four out of five French soldiers were peasants – seem in particular to have endured the war with patient resignation. They were more respectful of authority than urban workers but also more solitary and egotistical. Food was to them still an almost inexhaustible source of contentment. Bloch began with the assumption that peasants and workers would be uncouth, but found them often remarkably sensitive. He found himself more able to withstand bloody sights than they were.

The bloody sights were not susceptible to easy treatment. Shrapnel and high velocity bullets left hideous wounds which in the heat of battle could not be speedily treated. The wounded were then often infected by tetanus or gangrene. It took time to develop the range of techniques and skills (including X-rays) required to provide even a modicum of effective treatment. Although 'specialists' in various aspects of surgery emerged under the stimulus of need, there was, for example, no blood transfusion service available. Brain and plastic surgery made particularly rapid progress. 'Shell shock' became a recognized phenomenon, and for the first time psychiatrists were given an important role to play in its treatment. Fresh questions were inevitably raised about the boundary between 'illness' and 'cowardice'. New developments like gas and chemical warface in turn led to advances in pharmacology and biochemistry, as drugs were found to mitigate some of the effects.

Even more devastating, particularly in the Balkans and the Mediterranean, were the casualties caused by disease. Then there was alcohol. The British royal family was reluctantly persuaded to set an example by abstaining for the duration of the war, but the impact of this gesture was marginal. Observers testified to entire camps being on occasion 'drunk' and partiality to this condition was not confined to the British. Temperance groups in the United States were able to persuade the American war department to ban the sale of liquor near training camps. In theory at least, no man in uniform was able to buy a drink. All armies were concerned about venereal infection. Lord Kitchener had a pamphlet on the virtues of continence for the benefit of every soldier. Posters in American training camps suggested that 'A German Bullet is cleaner than a Whore'. Washington did not take up Clemenceau's offer to help establish licensed houses of prostitution for the benefit of American troops. It was clear, however, that these matters were ordered differently in France.

Whatever the cause, the statistics of the dead, diseased and deformed were stark enough, and perhaps most obtrusive in the case of France. It has been calculated that the dead of the French army, placed head to toe, would have formed an unbroken line from Berlin to Paris three times over – a total of 1.3 million, some 16 per cent of the number mobilized. All the major European states lost over 1 million dead – the Russians and the Germans losing nearly 2 million – though the French percentage was higher than any. The British empire figure did not quite reach 1 million, the Italian was about half a million, and the United States lost 114,000 – these last two suffering the smallest percentage of deaths to men mobilized. Over 2 million Frenchmen were wounded during the course of the war – about half of whom were subsequently to be in receipt of invalid pensions. About 50,000 were listed as possessing 100 per cent invalidity in the immediate postwar years. The *mutilés de guerre* were an only too common reminder of 1914–18 in postwar French life.

Confronted by such figures it might be thought surprising that so many armies stayed the course. There were murmurings and mutinies but, comparatively speaking, they were not very significant. The most notorious – though at the time great lengths were gone to in order to preserve secrecy – took place in the French army. In May 1917, various French regiments drawn from line infantry divisions who had suffered the heaviest casualties refused to obey orders, though it would seem that there was little co-ordinated action. It was also noted that the number of troops deserting had rapidly increased. The immediate cause of the disaffection was the failure of the Chemin des Dames offensive. Expectations of a successful offensive on this occasion had raised false hopes of an early end to the war. The lack of success led to the feeling that a breakthrough would be impossible. It was accompanied by a sense of hopelessness about the general direction of the war. There were also specific complaints about inadequate leave. Throughout late May and into early June revolts broke out in various units. One group of mutineers planned to seize a train at Soissons and drive it to Paris. One regiment simply withdrew into a wood and refused to come out. There was a disposition among generals to blame pacifist propaganda, but most of the demands implied that the men were willing to resume fighting if their requests for improved leave and conditions were met. Between May and November 1917 there were over 400 death-sentences in the armies under Pétain's command arising out of these incidents – the majority of them being subsequently commuted. Thousands of lesser punishments were meted out. In the months that followed, Pétain worked strenuously to contain the revolts by a mixture of firmness and readiness to show himself personally concerned about the welfare of his troops. The situation was grave, but it is important to remember that the numbers involved – 30/40,000 – constituted only a small section of the French army, even if the feelings to which they gave vent were more widely shared. The possibility that the army might disintegrate was something that Pétain could never afford to ignore.

In comparison, although there was a riot at the British camp at Étaples in September 1917, it arose out of particular local circumstances and when a particularly obnoxious training programme was modified the unrest died away. The British army as a whole was not in a mutinous condition. Nor was the German – until a very late stage. After the Bolshevik revolution, the maintenance of army discipline presented increasing problems – desertion was growing and returned captives from Russia were disinclined to see further service in the West. In September 1918 individual cases of mutiny were noted by the district command for Berlin. In the last few weeks of the war it was evident that many German soldiers no longer wished to continue the struggle, and small mutinies did occur. The naval mutiny at Kiel in early November spread to other Baltic ports. By then the war was coming to an end.

The multi-national character of their armies posed additional problems for Russia and Austria-Hungary, with the constant reality of reluctance to fight, in certain contexts, among Czechs, Poles or other nationalities. Yet even in the case of the Russian army it is an exaggeration to speak of its collapse. It was been suggested that in the first place this was an invention of Russian officers which then rebounded upon them. In November 1917 there were still some 6,500,000 men in the front area, though signs of demoralization are apparent in the number of men on the sick-list and who managed to remove themselves from the possibility of fighting. In his book on the Eastern front, Stone detects a profound duality in the condition of the Russian soldier at this juncture. He did not want to go on fighting yet remained patriotic. The accumulating failures of supply and food shortages finally issued in modest mutiny and corrosive desertion. It was not fighting and the war which led men to revolt against it, but the breakdown of the system on which they depended for *effective* fighting. The situation both in Germany and Russia could only lead to the eruption of hatred against officers. It was now time to pull out knives and kill them.

The commanders of the respective armies have fared little better at the hands of subsequent commentators. It has become commonplace to speak not of the wisdom of old generals but rather of their folly. Certainly old men did well out of the war. Kitchener was 64 when he was appointed war secretary and Fisher 73 when he returned as first sea lord. Such concern for the elderly, however, was not an insular peculiarity. Old soldiers (at the top) were straining at the leash everywhere. All the initial German non-royal army commanders at the outset of the war were in their late sixties. Moltke, the German chief of staff, was 66 and felt older. Some of these ripe paragons were to be put out to grass quite speedily, but that could not be said of the 67-year-old Paul von Beneckendorf und von Hindenburg, summoned out of retirement in 1914. Kitchener was lost at sea in 1916 on a trip to Russia; but it would be quite wrong to suggest that less adventurous generals kept a suitable distance from the reality of fighting. Some sixty British generals lost their lives on the Western front. There can be no resolution of the argument about the best position for a commander to occupy during a battle. And even if there could be, speculation would continue on the qualities to be looked for in generalship. The scale of suffering in the First World War prompts the easy reflection that generals were locked in a war of attrition and lacked the gifts which would enable them to find a way out. It has been frequently stated that they lacked imagination – as if imagination were a necessary quality in generals. More recently it has come to seem as if there was no swift and painless path to success that was only missed by obstinacy and stupidity. The war came at an awkward point – it introduced into the arena weapons and balances which offered no resolution except through endurance. It was still a conflict in which the values of pre-industrial military culture survived but in which it also became more apparent that their scope was constricted by the facts of technology and industrial might. Poets who sought *ein Heldenleben* by going to war found that it was merely the extension of the society they professed to loathe. No more than generals were they capable of speedy mental adjustment to the new reality. It is a curious commentary on the Europe of the submarine, the flying machine and the tank that in 1916 the Italian government was headed by the 78-year-old Boselli, the Russian by the 77-year-old I. L. Goremykin, and in 1917 the French by the 76-year-old Clemenceau. Such venerable figures could not but see in what was taking place the culmination of those struggles for national consolidation and unification which had dominated their political lives. It became apparent too that this encounter had to be all-embracing. The experience of war left little space for those who wished to be *au-dessus de la mêlée*.

Musicians, for the most part, were content to play their part in the creation of national harmony. Stanford drummed up a suitable accompaniment for Sir Henry Newbolt's *Song of the Sea*, swelling with the national pride of an Irishman in the cause of England. Elgar, promoted to Inspector in the Special Constabulary and shortly to swell the ranks of the Hampstead Volunteer Reserve, set *Carillon* by the Belgian poet Émile Cammaerts and, later, Kipling's *Firings of the Fleet*. Hubert Parry passed a tune (*the* tune) for Blake's *Jerusalem* to Walford Davies while they were attending a 'Fight for Right' meeting. Debussy meditated a *Marche héroique* but felt that it ill-accorded with his own comfortable sedentary circumstances. However, his *Berceuse héroique* proved an admirable substitute, being first published in that tribute to gallant Belgium, *King Albert's Book*. Prokofiev, the only son of a widow and therefore exempt from military service, settled down to composing, possibly appropriately, *The Ugly Duckling*. Stravinsky happened to be in Switzerland and decided, like other Russians, that it was a sensible place to be. Rachmaninov composed his *Night Vigil* – with all profits to war victims. The Bolshevik revolution did not prove congenial and he left Russia in 1917. The singer Chaliapin sent him on his way with a packet of caviar and a loaf of homemade white bread. Schoenberg, with his customary thoroughness, disappeared into military uniform and thought it quite inappropriate to talk about music. Martinů, like his country, emerged from obscurity in January 1919 to have his patriotic cantata *Czech Rhapsody* played in Prague. Janáček had already written a suitable chorus for male voices – *The Czech Legion*. Richard Strauss spent a lot of the war bemoaning the fact that the British government had confiscated his savings of thirty years, which he had trustingly left with Sir Edgar Speyer to invest in London. Sir Edgar, the subject of much adverse criticism because of his German-Jewish origins, could not help, because he decided to flee to the United States. Eighty virtuous French musicians, including Saint-Saëns, signed a memorial prepared by the National League for the Defence of French Music (1916) urging a ban on the works of all German and Austrian composers not yet in the public domain. Ravel, whose signature was requested, declined. However, he did have a problem. He was patriotic and insisted on fighting, despite poor health, but he happened to be composing a piece which he had provisionally entitled *Wien*. That no longer seemed appropriate, but *Petrograd* did not quite fit the bill. He eventually settled for *La Valse*.

Christians were active too. The war was well advanced when Sir Douglas Haig remarked to the assistant chaplain general to the British First Army 'Tell your chaplains that a good chaplain is as valuable as a good General', presuming that the value of a good general was self-evident. The commitment most clergy felt to the war at its outbreak remained undimmed as its dimensions unfolded. Nor were the intellectual laity reticent in their support. No Christian, wrote the Anglican philosopher C. C. J. Webb, could regard suffering as utterly evil. It was not the case that the worst peace was better than the best war. He supposed that all through history hitherto, God had used war as a main instrument in the moulding of mankind. Ernest Barker, the political philosopher, thought that England belonged to Christ's Church Militant – therein lay her strength. In all European belligerent countries there was no difficulty in finding sufficient priests and pastors for chaplaincy work. There were only 113 at the beginning of the war serving with British forces but that figure had reached 3,480 by the armistice. More than a sprinkling of medals were distributed among them and about a hundred were killed. They did not all spend their time organizing amateur theatricals. As commissioned officers, padres sometimes found themselves in a somewhat awkward status in relation to 'men'. A view developed that Roman Catholic chaplains were endowed with a serenity which 'bluff Anglicans' lacked. Guy Chapman wrote in his autobiography that before sending men into action the Church of England's spiritual sustenance was a cigarette. Despite his nickname of 'Woodbine

Willie', however, the Revd G. A. Studdert Kennedy offered a good deal more than that. He visited the troops with a champion boxer, two champion wrestlers and an NCO who had killed eighteen Germans (on different occasions) with a bayonet. After his companions had demonstrated their respective skills, the padre finished off with a powerful twenty-minute sermon. On this high note, battle commenced.

Such idiosyncrasies were not peculiar to the Church of England. The religious pastorate was deemed to have a specially important role in the Austrian army in stressing the duty of soldiers to serve their emperor. It was a task that was eagerly undertaken. Likewise, German regiments were blessed in church before going off to the front. Whatever their actual beliefs, if any, the fallen were buried beneath the sign of the cross. One of the most popular wartime German writers declared that the sacrificial death of the German people was only a repetition, willed by God, of the death of Christ. In Germany, Catholics were particularly anxious to demonstrate their loyalty to the state and in their circles it was not uncommon to find the war described as the new springtime of religion. For similar reasons, French priests took a particularly active role in the French army. Perhaps 80,000 priests from all countries took part in the war and about half of this total were French. On the eve of American entry into the war, a Brooklyn Congregational minister offered as his idea of happiness the sight of the Kaiser, Tirpitz and Hindenburg hanging by a rope. It would be time to forgive the Germans when they were all shot. Undeterred, the Kaiser saw the hand of God in German progress in the Baltic and gave thanks accordingly.

It would be misleading to suppose that the merits of peace were entirely neglected. It appeared, however, that any initiative could only come from churchmen in neutral countries. The Lutheran archbishop of Uppsala appealed to the churches of the world in September 1914 to keep constantly before those in authority the ideal of peace. The archbishop of Canterbury declined to endorse the appeal, suggesting that it was imperative to bring to an issue 'the fundamental principle of faithfulness to a nation's obligation to its solemnly plighted word'. Indeed, for the duration of the war, with only minor exceptions, the leaders of the national churches of belligerent Europe, Orthodox and protestant, shared to the full their national perceptions of the issues at stake and the solidarity that was required.

The Vatican was in a somewhat different position, though its room for manœuvre was very limited. Pius X had died on the day the Germans entered Brussels – a mere coincidence rather than an expression of heartbreak. His successor, Benedict XV, an Italian, described war in his first message as 'the scourge of the wrath of God' and refused to allow chaplains to appear in military uniform within the Vatican. Italy's own stance placed the papacy in great difficulty and the weight of the Church on the whole favoured neutrality, but it did not prevail. Erzberger, the German Catholic leader, suggested to the pope that he might like an access to the sea if it were possible to keep Italy out of the war. He does not seem to have mentioned a Dreadnought as a further incentive. It was not until December 1916 that the pope called upon the belligerents to state their terms for peace. Then, after months of diplomatic preparation, on 1 August 1917 he issued an appeal for an end to hostilities, declaring that Europe was rushing into the abyss, as if stricken by universal madness, and committing suicide. The Western Powers saw in this action a special concern for Austria-Hungary – Pius X had indeed privately considered Austria's war against Serbia 'wholly just'. The Kaiser, in a very protestant mood as he celebrated four hundred years of the Reformation, was not pleased by the intervention either. A substantial section of the French faithful regarded Benedict XV as the 'Boche pope' and his initiative was denounced in a sermon by a celebrated preacher in La Madeleine. It was obvious that the papacy did not have sufficient authority to promote a negotiation. For the most part, Catholics in Europe did not waver in their patriotic commitment and did not see the pope as a possible instrument of political reconciliation. Of none was this more true than Cardinal Mercier of Belgium who seemed to equate piety with loyalty to the French-speaking Belgian unitary state.

Just as a Swedish episcopal appeal fell on deaf ears, so the inter-belligerent labour conference scheduled for Stockholm never took place. The idea of such a gathering had come from the Petrograd soviet and would have brought together socialists who had opposed the war and socialists who supported it. Various obstacles were placed in the way of the French and British delegations and they never arrived. German socialists both from the SPD and the newly founded USPD were divided in their estimate of what might have been achieved. Some took the view that it would only have been a gathering of those who could do nothing effective for peace and who would divide at the first opportunity, while others were more optimistic. Socialists constantly reiterated the view that war was the means by which capitalism attempted to avoid revolution by appealing to national unity. Even if this unlikely hypothesis were accepted, it had to be admitted that the appeal seemed largely successful. An ideological appeal to a socialism which was as doctrinally and institutionally fragmented as Christianity could not stop the war. Nevertheless, a small group of socialists met at Zimmerwald in Switzerland in September 1915 – among them Lenin – and declared that they rejected the principle of national solidarity with the exploiters and accepted only the international solidarity of the proletariat and the class struggle. But they were deeply divided. Some wanted the emphasis placed upon immediate peace, others, including Lenin, were more interested in the revolutionary possibilities that the continuance of the war might present. A further conference, also in Switzerland, warned governments in a May Day message in 1916 that in all countries hatred of war was increasing and the will to social vengeance was growing. It was believed that only when these two feelings were united would the hour of peace dawn. Eighteen months later Lenin was to achieve this feat in Russia but even so the working classes in the rest of Europe either could not or would not do the same. The representative of the American Federation of Labour arrived at the Inter-Allied Labour and socialist conference in September 1918 armed with strict instructions from his boss, Samuel Gompers, to make sure that no inter-belligerent conference took place. 'Don't call a spade a spade, call it a son-of-a-bitch', were the orders, 'Fuck them'. On this basis, it would still take time for the workers of the world to liberate themselves from their national chains.

One notable fact about the experience of war was that it was a world dominated by men. Some German feminists in October 1914 pointed out that it was the fault of men that the gruesome war had begun. True humanity did not recognize the hatred of nation against nation and women stood closer to humanity than men. The achievement of the suffrage would only be the prelude to a radical transformation of society. Echoes of these sentiments were to be found in all belligerent countries. Women understood about birth and death in a fashion foreign to men. It might be necessary to struggle against men in order to defeat their wars. Yet there was a quite contrary argument, part tactical and part strategic. The war gave women a distinctive opportunity to demonstrate that they could operate in roles from which they had hitherto been largely excluded. Success in these spheres would show how antiquated and irrelevant were current masculine stereotypes. The pathway to political acceptance would then be open. Patriotic sentiment, however, was more than a device to a particular end. For every woman who resented war as an activity of men there was another who resented the exclusive rights over fighting which men seemed to exercise. Although the initial assumption was that middle-class women would find their vocation as nurses, the 'bourgeois' Russian empress and her elder daughters providing the supreme example, there was more and more work in Germany, France and Britain for women in the munitions factories and other war-related sectors of industry. There were, for example, 125 women working at Woolwich Arsenal in 1914 and 25,000 in 1917. Three and a quarter million British women were employed in July 1914 and a little under 5 million at the close of the war – the expansion being most rapid in the middle years. In France by late 1918 half a million women were directly working in war industries and some 150,000 occupied secretarial and other ancillary positions in the army. Both of these figures represented a major change from the position in 1914.

Yet amongst women there seems to have been no general expectation that this change of occupation would be permanent – though even temporary changes on this scale led to awkward questions being asked about equal pay, which trade union officials found scarcely more congenial than their employers did. There was, however, one lasting victory. It did prove possible for Land Girls and others who wore trousers at work to wear them off duty, despite 'reasonable' attempts to prevent them doing so. In any event it was the untrousered over-30s whom the British government saw fit to reward with the vote in 1918. By that stage, the losses sustained in war made it apparent that there was important work ahead for women. Perhaps it was the case that the factory turned their sex into one united family – a surrogate experience for the trenches, it was claimed – but when peace returned there was an undoubted need for the reproduction of real families. Dynamism in this respect was already conspicuously absent in prewar France but, for obvious reasons, 1916 saw the lowest annual number of recorded births in French population history. Better leave-arrangements did something to rectify the position, but it was still a matter of anxiety, not statistically relieved by the fact that the war seems to have caused a marked reduction in the annual suicide rate. It is also to be noted that French warriors were preparing for the future by mysteriously arranging that their wives achieved a 1 per cent increase during the war years in the proportion of baby boys to baby girls. Perhaps the Countess of Warwick had foreseen such developments when she wrote in 1916 of woman as the saviour of the race. 'I see her fruitful womb replenish the wasted ranks', she declared, 'I hear her wise counsels making irresistibly attractive the flower-strewn ways of peace.'

There were, however, at least two men in Europe in 1918 for whom the experience of war had not been such that in future they would restrict themselves to saying it with flowers: Adolf Hitler and Benito Mussolini. The former had been classified in February 1914 as 'unfit for military service', but such scruples were waived by the authorities six months later. In October he was serving with the Bavarian Volunteer Regiment in Flanders, where it immediately sustained heavy casualties. Hitler was awarded the Iron Cross Second Class – and later received further decorations. He was twice wounded but gained the reputation of having a charmed life. It seems that his comrades found his zeal a little tiresome. Five months of sick leave in Munich convinced him that the home population was failing to understand the spirit of the front-line soldier and the enormity of the issues at stake for Germany. Mussolini, like Hitler, was promoted to corporal, though he would have liked to have gone higher. Unlike Hitler, he was a considerable figure in Italian public life, his decision to support the war having caused a furore in left-wing circles. It soon became clear to him that the Italian war effort was not quite the Garibaldian adventure which he had talked of, but there was material in the experience of men in the front line to create a new political movement. Apparently, he was already talking in 1916 of *trincero-crazia*, of the men from the trenches who would determine the future. The experience of war was not to be over for mankind after all.

Since the war frequently remained, for those who had fought, the most important event in their lives, it was tempting to find in it the proximate cause of the most significant social, political, economic and cultural developments over the ensuing twenty years. It was and is said that the war altered the course of European history. At one level, the suggestion is almost a truism. In so far as European states had spent years attempting to destroy each other, the cumulative consequence, over time, was to undermine the position of Europe as a whole in the world. There were strenuous and not altogether unsuccessful attempts to pretend, in the decades that followed, that Europe remained the hub of the universe, but it was an illusion which could not be sustained indefinitely. It may now seem tempting to speculate on what role Europe might have played in the subsequent development of the world if conflict had been avoided – especially since, at this distance, the alleged 'issues' at stake, apart indeed from the concern for national supremacy, do not seem so manifestly 'moral' as those which divided the combatants (or some of them) in the Second World War or other subsequent conflicts.

When other specific aspects are considered, it is not easy to draw up a convincing way of measuring the impact of war and deciding the extent to which it inaugurated, accelerated or determined the fate of structures and movements. Arguably, the war speeded up the collapse of the Habsburg, Romanov and Ottoman empires. Their demise had long been predicted, but they had shown great resilience and denied their critics the satisfaction of seeing their prophecies come true before 1914. Their cohesion during the war was greater than many observers had anticipated. Without the additional pressures of war, their chances of survival, at least for some decades, might have been greater.

War likewise gave the Bolsheviks in Russia an opportunity to take power which might otherwise have eluded them for ever. The British Liberal party might not have disintegrated. There might not have been a rising in Dublin at Eastertime in 1916. And so on. Some of these 'counter-factual' speculations have a fascination precisely because they admit of no final answer. Certainly, while there was a burst of revolutionary activity throughout Europe in the immediate aftermath of war, a development consonant with the socially disruptive and dislocative effects of warfare, such activity was, for the most part, unsuccessful. It was the energy devoted to the 'recasting of bourgeois Europe' which brought lasting, if somewhat precarious, results. The intention was to return to 'normal', and to see 1914–18 as an aberration rather than as an event of such dimensions that no restoration was possible. Votes for women did indeed come to Britain, in two stages, after having been strenuously resisted before 1914, but it is too simple to regard these measures as merely a display of thanks or a recognition of services rendered during the war. It is just as plausible to see in female suffrage a realization of the fact that women posed no threat, as such, to the political system. Indeed, more generally, it proved remarkably easy to phase many women out of occupations that they had temporarily filled when men were otherwise engaged.

And in literature and painting, music and drama, philosophy and theology, it is difficult to see the war as inspiring developments and ideas for which there was no prewar precedent or parallel. What was perhaps significant was that the feelings of rootlessness and nihilism apparent in intellectual circles before 1914 had a wider resonance in 1919 than would have been the case but for the war. Even here, however, it is dangerous to exaggerate the difficulty men felt in returning to their old homes and habits. What also became more general was a certain scepticism about the inevitability either of 'progress' or of the manifestation of the Kingdom of God on earth. Yet the prophets of doom and disaster were as much confounded as those who talked romantically about the homes for heroes. It was the ability of European states to recover their strength which was most striking. War forced men to find more efficient ways of administration and industrial organization and to concern themselves with improvements in health and welfare. The thrust of technological and scientific development had been dramatic, with totally unexpected benefits and complications. The pace of change in these respects only marginally slackened and further revolutions in transport and mass-communications were imminent. In this sense, the dynamism which had been so characteristic of pre-1914 Europe soon reasserted itself, though it also carried with it the danger of promethean ambition and a further armed struggle for mastery.

In 1919, that contest seemed to most people a remote contingency. For the time being, the bruised and battered earth was bandaged and restored. Huge numbers of crosses peopled the silent landscape. From all over the world, in years to come, relatives and friends trooped through these incommunicative cities of the dead. The cemeteries of Europe housed them, for, in the end, there was little to be said for trying to bring the fallen home. 'It is just as near from France to heaven as from Indiana,' concluded one mother. There could be no better comment on the fate of those who left their homes to fight in the First World War.

Further Reading

General

There have been many hundreds of books on the war. The emphasis in this guide is upon those published in the last twenty years, since the bibliographies which many of them contain give adequate reference to earlier volumes. There are numerous single-volume histories, though the emphasis in most of them is upon military developments. B. H. Liddell Hart's *A History of the First World War*, 1970, having been first published under a different title forty years earlier, merits the accolade 'classic'. His successors include: C. B. Falls, *The First World War*, 1960; A. J. P. Taylor, *The First World War*, 1963; M. Ferro, *The Great War, 1914–1918*, 1973, a translation from the French original published in 1969; H. Baldwin, *World War I*, New York, 1962, is a short history; J. L. Stokesbury, *A Short History of World War I*, 1982, is quite long. D. J. Goodspeed, *The German Wars, 1914–1945*, 1977, attempts a general account of both contests. There is a mass of detailed information in V. J. Esposito, ed., *A Concise History of World War I*, New York, 1964. J. C. King, ed., *The First World War*, New York, 1972, is a documentary collection with helpful commentary. G. Hardach, *The First World War 1914–1918*, 1977, is the most useful economic history of the war.

Good maps are available in M. Gilbert, *First World War Atlas*, 1971; A. Banks, *A Military Atlas of the First World War*, 1975.

M. Howard, *War in European History*, Oxford, 1976, puts the events of 1914 in a wider context and there are also stimulating discussions in his *Studies in War and Peace*, 1970, and *War and the Liberal Conscience*, 1978. Certain essays in his *The Causes of War*, 1983, are also relevant. W. H. McNeill, *The Pursuit of Power: technology, armed force and society since AD 1000*, Oxford, 1983, is an illuminating reflection on the causes and consequences of war throughout history.

Two valuable bibliographies are: G. M. Baylis, *Bibliographic Guide to the Two World Wars*, Epping, 1977; *A Subject Bibliography of the First World War, books in English 1914–1978*, Aldershot, 1979.

Chapter 1

No war has been more extensively studied in its causes than that of 1914.

F. Fischer's work, translated into English somewhat misleadingly as *Germany's Aims in the First World War*, 1967, had a major impact on interpretation. His own reflections on the debates that ensued can be found in *World Power or Decline: the controversy over Germany's aims in the First World War*, 1975. H. W. Koch, ed., *The Origins of the First World War*, 1972, is a useful collection of articles, among them being J. Joll's influential lecture 'Unspoken Assumptions'. A. J. P. Taylor, *War by Time-Table: How the First World War Began*, 1969, is a brisk account. L. C. F. Turner, *Origins of the First World War*, 1970, is a short introduction. R. Langhorne, *The Collapse of the Concert of Europe: International Politics, 1890–1914*, 1981, is a thoughtful essay. V. R. Berghahn, *Germany and the Approach of War in 1914*, 1973, and Z. S. Steiner, *Britain and the Origins of the First World War*, 1977, are both excellent studies and augur well for volumes on other countries in the Makers of the Twentieth Century series. F. H. Hinsley, ed., *The Foreign Policy of Sir Edward Grey*, Cambridge, 1977, contains a wide range of studies on British policy and an extensive bibliography. R. J. B. Bosworth, *Italy, the least of the Great Powers: Italian foreign policy before the First World War*, Cambridge, 1979, is a detailed volume. V. Dedijer examined *The Road to Sarajevo*, 1967. M. B. Petrovich has written the most recent *History of Modern Serbia*, 1976. F. R. Bridge, *From Sadowa to Sarajevo*, 1972, considers the foreign policy of Austria-Hungary. J. Heller, *British Policy towards the Ottoman Empire, 1908–1914*, 1983, is a thorough study of a neglected aspect of prewar diplomacy. B. Tuchman, *August 1914*, 1962, and *The Proud Tower*, 1967, provide atmosphere. Helpful on relations between particular Great Powers are R. Bridge, *Great Britain and Austria-Hungary, 1906–1914*, 1972, and P. M. Kennedy, *The Rise of the Anglo-German antagonism, 1890–1914*, 1980. A. J. Mayer, *The Persistence of the Old Regime: Europe to the Great War*, 1981, is a stimulating examination of the mind and mood of Europe. Planning for war, part of that mental activity, can be examined in P. M. Kennedy, ed., *The War Plans of the Great Powers, 1880–1914*, 1979; also relevant is L. L. Farrar, *The Short-War Illusion*, Oxford, 1973.

Reactions to the outbreak of war can be studied in J. J. Becker, *1914: comment les Français sont entrés dans la guerre*, Paris, 1977; R. Stromberg, 'Redemption by War: the Intellectuals and 1914', *Midwest Quarterly*, 20 no. 3, 1979; S. Bernstein, 'L'opinion française au miroir de la guerre', *Revue d'histoire moderne et contemporaine*, xxvi, 1979; general discussion of attitudes towards war and peace can be found in A. Vagts, *The History of Militarism*, 1959; V. R. Berghahn, *Militarism*, Leamington Spa, 1982; I. F. Clarke, *Voices prophesying war, 1763–1984*, 1966; P. Brock, *Pacifism in Europe to 1914*, Princeton, 1972; K. G. Robbins, *The Abolition of War: the 'Peace Movement' in Britain, 1914–1919*, Cardiff, 1976; M. Ceadel, *Pacifism in Britain, 1914–1945*, Oxford, 1980; R. Chickering, *Imperial Germany and a*

World without War: the Peace Movement and German Society, 1892-1914, Princeton, 1975, also contains a chapter on pacifism in France. Reactions to war amongst churches and socialist parties can be found in J. D. Holmes, *The Papacy in the Modern World*, 1981; J. S. Curtis, *Church and State in Russia: the last years of the Empire, 1900-1917*, New York, 1972 reprint; A. Dansette, *The Religious History of Modern France*, 1961; A. Marrin, *The Last Crusade: the Church of England in the First World War*, Durham, N. C., 1974; K. Hammer, *Deutsche Kriegstheologie, 1870-1918*, Munich, 1974; J. Joll, *The Second International*, 1974 edition; G. Haupt, *Socialism and the Great War*, Oxford, 1972; useful studies on the world outside Europe include R. Storry, *Japan and the Decline of the West in Asia, 1898-1943*, 1978; P. Lowe, *Britain and the Far East*, 1981; M. Crowder, *West Africa under Colonial Rule*, 1968; vol. xix of the *Journal of African History* is devoted entirely to Africa and the First World War; S. J. and E. K. Shaw, *History of the Ottoman Empire and Modern Turkey*, vol. 2, Cambridge, 1977; B. Lewis, *The Emergence of Modern Turkey*, 1968; B. C. Busch, *Britain, India and the Arabs, 1914-1921*, Berkeley, Calif., 1971; M. R. D. Foot, ed., *War and Society*, 1973, includes interesting essays on dominion attitudes and on India. B. C. Busch, *Hardinge of Penshurst*, Hamden, Conn., 1980, reveals the mind of the first wartime viceroy. Small European countries are normally ignored but there is detail in G. B. Leon, *Greece and the Great Powers, 1914-1917*, Thessalonika, 1974; O. Riste, *The Neutral Ally*, 1965 (concerns Norway); E. H. Kossmann, *The Low Countries, 1780-1940*, Oxford, 1978; J. E. Helmreich, *Belgium and Europe: a study in small-power diplomacy*, The Hague, 1976; T. Kaarsted, *Great Britain and Denmark, 1914-1920*, Odense, 1979; V. S. Vardys and R. J. Misiunas, *The Baltic States in Peace and War, 1917-1945*, 1978. Biographies of some of the leading European political figures in 1914 include H. Hantsch, *Leopold Graf Berchtold*, Graz, 1963; K. Jarausch, *The Enigmatic Chancellor: Bethmann Hollweg and the Hubris of Imperial Germany*, New Haven, 1973; P. Miquel, *Poincaré*, Paris, 1961, A. W. Palmer, *The Kaiser*, 1978; J. C. G. Röhl and N. Sombart, eds, *Kaiser Wilhelm II: new interpretations*, Cambridge, 1982; K. G. Robbins, *Sir Edward Grey*, 1971.

Chapter 2

G. Ritter, *The Schlieffen Plan*, 1958; J. Terraine, *Mons: Retreat to Victory*, 1960; T. Carew, *The Vanished Army*, 1964, deals with the original British Expeditionary Force; A. Clark, *The Donkeys*, 1961; A. H. Farrar-Hockley, *The Somme*, 1964; M. Middlebrook, *The First Day of the Somme*, 1971; A. Horne, *The Price of Glory: Verdun 1916*, 1962; R. Watt, *Dare Call it Treason*, New York, 1963; H. Essame, *The Battle for Europe, 1918*, New York, 1972; B. Pitt, *The Last Act*, 1962; J. Toland, *No Man's Land: the Story of 1918*, 1980. This selection of books concerns aspects of the war in Western Europe. The following consider some other episodes: A. W. Palmer, *The Gardeners of Salonika*, 1965; R. Millar, *Kut*, 1969; A. Moorehead, *Gallipoli*, 1956; R. R. James, *Gallipoli*, 1965; C. Miller, *Battle for the Bundu: the First World War in East Africa*, New York, 1974; C. B. Burdick, *The Japanese Siege of Tsingtau*, Hamden, Conn., 1976. N. Stone, *The Eastern Front, 1914–1917*, 1976, is indispensable for this theatre.

Chapter 3

National naval histories are discussed in A. J. Marder, *From the Dreadnought to Scapa Flow: the Royal Navy in the Fisher era, 1904–1919*, 5 vols., 1961–70; P. M. Kennedy, *The Rise and Fall of British Naval Mastery*, 1976; D. W. Mitchell, *A History of Russian and Soviet Sea Power*, 1974. The general naval history of the war is best approached through G. Bennett, *Naval Battles of the First World War*, 1968, and G. Jordan, ed., *Naval Warfare in the Twentieth Century, 1900–1943*, 1977. Two naval campaigns are analysed in G. Bennett, *Coronel and the Falklands*, 1962, and D. MacIntyre, *Jutland*, 1957. E. Horton, *The Illustrated History of the Submarine*, 1974, discusses the evolution of this new menace and R. M. Grant, *U-boats Destroyed: the effect of anti-submarine warfare, 1914–1918*, 1964. Different light on the war at sea is revealed by D. Horn, *The German Naval Mutinies of World War I*, N. Brunswick, N. J., 1969, and E. Mawdsley, *The Russian Revolution and the Baltic Sea Fleet*, 1978. Various British naval heroes appear in A. T. Patterson, *Jellicoe*, 1969; R. F. Mackay, *Fisher of Kilverstone*, Oxford, 1974; S. Roskill, *Earl Beatty: the first naval hero*, 1980.

J. Gooch, *Armies in Europe*, 1980, offers a helpful general introduction. The French military machine can be further considered in R. D. Challener, *The French Theory of the Nation in Arms, 1866–1939*, New York, 1955, and P. de la Gorce, *The French Army*, 1963. N. Stone, 'Army and Society in the Habsburg Monarchy, 1900–1914', *Past and Present*, 33, April 1966, is an illuminating article. There is reliable background in E. M. Spiers, *The Army and Society, 1815–1914*, 1980, which deals with the United Kingdom. Military matters obtrude into J. Whittam, *The Politics of the Italian Army, 1861–1918*, 1977. On the German army there is no lack of material: M. Kitchen, *A Military History of Germany*, 1975; M. Kitchen, *The German Officer Corps, 1890–1914*, Oxford, 1968; V. R. Berghahn and M. Kitchen, eds, *Germany in the Age of Total War*, 1981. Logistical and other technical aspects are considered in M. van Creveld, *Supplying War*, Cambridge, 1977, and N. F. Dreisziger, ed., *Mobilization for Total War*, Waterloo, Ont., 1981. Mechanical aspects are discussed in J. Ellis, *The Social History of the Machine Gun*, 1975; B. Fitzsimons, *Tanks and Weapons of the First World War*, New York, 1973; S. Bidwell and D. Graham, *Fire-Power: British Army Weapons and Theories of War 1904–1945*, 1982.

The evolution of the use of aircraft in war is described in B. Collier, *A History of Air Power*, 1974; R. Higham, *Air Power*, 1972; A. Clark, *Aces High: the War in the Air over the Western Front, 1914–1918*, 1973; C. Bowyer, *Airmen of World War I*, 1975; D. Winter, *The First of the Few*, 1982; H. G. Castle, *Fire over England: The German Air Raids in World War I*, 1982; C. H. Gibbs-Smith, *Aviation: an historical survey from its origins to World War II*, 1970.

Chapter 4

Studies of 'war aims' and diplomacy have become steadily more comprehensive with the increased availability of documents. Relatively early studies include: W. W. Gottlieb, *Studies in Secret Diplomacy*, 1957; Z. A. B. Zeman, *A Diplomatic History of the First World War*, 1971; A. J. Mayer, *Political Origins of the New Diplomacy, 1917–1918*, New Haven, 1959. British aims are considered in P. Guinn, *British Strategy and Politics, 1914 to 1918*, 1965; V. H. Rothwell, *British War Aims and Peace Diplomacy, 1914–1918*, Oxford, 1971; G. W. Egerton, *Great Britain and the Creation of the League of Nations*, Chapel Hill, 1978; K. J. Calder, *Britain and the Origins of the New Europe, 1914–1918*, Cambridge, 1976; C. and H. Seton-Watson, *The Making of a New Europe: R. W. Seton-Watson and the last years of Austria-Hungary*, 1980. There is material on French aims in W. A. McDougall, *France's Rhineland and Diplomacy, 1914–1924*, Princeton, 1978; D. Stevenson, *French War Aims against Germany, 1914–1919*, Oxford, 1982; M. Trachtenberg, *Reparation in World Politics: France and European Economic Diplomacy, 1916–1923*, New York, 1980; C. M. Andrew and A. S. Kanya-Forstner, *France Overseas: the Great War and the Climax of French Imperial Expansion*, 1982. There is material on Italy in C. Seton-Watson, *Italy from Liberalism to Fascism, 1870–1923*, 1967; J. A. Thayer, *Italy and the Great War: Politics and Culture, 1870–1915*, Madison, Wisc., 1964. There is material on Russia in C. J. Smith, *The Russian Struggle for Power, 1914–1917: a study of Russian Foreign Policy during the First World War*, New York, 1956. F. G. Weber, *Eagles on the Crescent: Germany, Austria and the Diplomacy of the Turkish Alliance, 1914–1918* tackles less familiar ground. R. A. Kann, B. K. Kiraly and P. S. Fichtner, eds, consider *The Habsburg Empire in World War I*, New York, 1977, while W. Fest, *Peace or Partition: The Habsburg Monarchy and British Policy, 1914–1918*, 1982, is the latest of a number of books on this theme.

Chapter 5

The military–civil relationship can be traced in P. Dennis and A. Preston, eds, *Soldiers as Statesmen*, 1976; B. Brodie, *War and Politics*, 1973; A. J. P. Taylor, *Politics in Wartime*, 1964; Lord Hankey, *The Supreme Command*,

1914-1918, 1961; J. C. King, *Generals and Politicians: Conflict between France's Command, Parliament and Government, 1914-1918*, Berkeley and Los Angeles, 1951; M. Kitchen, *The Silent Dictatorship: the Politics of the German High Command under Hindenburg and Ludendorff, 1916-1918*, 1976; K. Burk, ed., *The War and the State: the Transformation of British Government, 1914-1919*, 1982; J. Turner, *Lloyd George's Secretariat*, Cambridge, 1979; P. Renouvin, *The Forms of War Government in France*, 1927; D. R. Watson, *Georges Clemenceau: a political biography*, 1974; G. Pedroncini, *Pétain: Général en Chef, 1917-1918*, Paris, 1974; R. Griffiths, *Pétain*, 1972: more generals can be studied in V. Bonham-Carter, *Soldier True: the life and times of Field Marshal Sir William Robertson*, 1963; R. Hough, *The Little Field Marshal: Sir John French*, 1981; J. Terraine, *Haig: the educated soldier*, 1960: opposition to the war is discussed by J. Vellacott, *Bertrand Russell and the Pacifists of the First World War*, Brighton, 1980; J. Rae, *Conscience and Politics: the British Government and the Conscientious Objection to Military Service, 1916-1919*, 1970; F. L. Carsten, *War against War: British and German Radical Movements in the First World War*, 1982: Gandhi's position is treated in J. M. Brown, *Gandhi's Rise to Power: Indian Politics, 1915-1922*, Cambridge, 1972. H. C. Peterson and G. C. Fite, *Opponents of War, 1917-1918*, 1968, consider American objectors: an old book by J. D. Squires, *British Propaganda at Home and in the United States from 1914 to 1917*, Cambridge, Mass., 1935, can be supplemented by C. Haste, *Keep the Home Fires Burning: Propaganda in the First World War*, 1977, M. Sanders and P. M. Taylor, *British Propaganda during the First World War, 1914-18*, 1983, and P. M. Taylor, *The Projection of Britain*, Cambridge, 1981.

Numerous books consider American neutrality and intervention in 1917, among the most recent being P. Devlin, *Too Proud to Fight: Woodrow Wilson's neutrality*, 1974; E. M. Coffman, *The War to end all Wars: The American Military Experience in World War I*, New York, 1969, and F. E. Vandirer, *Black Jack: The Life and Times of John J. Pershing*, College Station, Texas, 1977, deal with military aspects; and F. C. Luebke, *Bonds of Loyalty: German-Americans and World War I*, DeKalb, 1974, and D. M. Kennedy, *Over Here: the First World War and American Society*, Oxford, 1980, consider domestic aspects. It is not appropriate to give a detailed bibliography of the events in Russia in 1917 but S. Fitzpatrick, *The Russian Revolution*, Oxford, 1982, and G. Katkov, *Russia 1917: the Kornilov Affair*, 1980, should be mentioned.

Chapter 6

The experience of war, as reflected in the works of writers, is a popular theme: P. Fussell, *The Great War and Modern Memory*, 1975, is particularly illuminating; K. Vondung, ed., *Kriegserlebnis. Der erste Weltkrieg in der literarischen Gestaltung und symbolischen Deutung der Nationen*, Göttingen, 1980, is an excellent collection of articles; also of value are B. Gardner, *Up the Line to Death: the War Poets, 1914–1918*, 1964; J. Silkin, *Out of Battle: the Poetry of the Great War*, 1972; J. Silkin, ed., *The Penguin Book of First World War Poetry*, Harmondsworth, 1979; F. Field, *Three French Writers and the Great War*, Cambridge, 1975; R. Wohl, *The Generation of 1914*, 1980; J. Cruickshank, *Variations on Catastrophe: some French responses to the Great War*, Oxford, 1982. M. Girouard takes the reader for a ride in *The Return to Camelot: Chivalry and the English Gentleman*, 1981. P. Vansittart, *Voices from the Great War*, 1981, H. Klein, ed., *The First World War in Fiction*, 1976 and G. A. Panichas, ed., *Promise of Greatness: the War of 1914–18*, 1968 all illuminate literary reactions.

A crop of recent studies focus on the context of fighting: E. J. Leed, *No Man's Land: Combat and Identity in World War I*, Cambridge, 1979; J. Keegan, *The Face of Battle*, 1976; C. Messenger, *Trench Fighting, 1914–1918*, 1972; T. Ashworth, *Trench Warfare 1914–1918*, 1980; M. Hanlihan, *World War I: Trench Warfare*, 1974; D. Winter, *Death's Men: Soldiers of the Great War*, 1978; S. R. Ward, ed., *The War Generation*, 1975; J. Baynes, *Morale: a study of men and courage*, 1967. The literature on humour and the war is sparse, but see H. Lauder, *A Minstrel in France*, New York, 1918. Historians at war include E. L. Woodward, *Short Journey*, 1942; M. Bloch, *Memories of War, 1914–15*, 1980, and the American profession is studied in G. T. Blakey, *Historians on the Home Front: American Propagandists for the Great War*, Lexington, 1970.

Demographic aspects are considered in C. Dyer, *Population and Society in Twentieth Century France*, 1978; J. M. Winter, 'The Demographic Consequences of World War I', *Population Studies*, 1976; R. Mitchison, *British Population Change since 1860*, 1977.

Further light on conscience emerges from W. Huber and G. Liedke, eds, *Christentum und Militarismus*, Stuttgart, 1974; G. Studdert-Kennedy, *Dog-Collar Democracy*, 1982; G. F. A. Best, *Humanity in Warfare: The Modern History of the International Law of Armed Conflicts*, 1980; M. Howard, ed., *Restraints on War*, Oxford, 1979. G. L. Mosse, *The Jews and the German War Experience, 1914–1918*, New York, 1977, is a fascinating exploration of identity. The role of women is considered in R. J. Evans, *The Feminist Movement in Germany, 1894–1933*, 1976; G. Braybon, *Women Workers in the First World War: the British experience*, 1981; A. Marwick, *Women at War, 1914–1918*, 1977. The war experience of two future warriors can be found in J. P. Stern, *Hitler: the Führer and the People*, Hassocks, 1975; A. J. Gregor, *Young Mussolini and the Intellectual Origins of Fascism*, 1979.

Biographical Notes

ALBERT, KING OF THE BELGIANS (1875–1934). Reigns from 1909 until his death. Active commander-in-chief of the Belgian army during the war.

H. H. ASQUITH (1852–1928). British chancellor of the exchequer, 1905–8; prime minister in the Liberal governments, 1908–15; Coalition prime minister, May 1915–December 1916, when replaced by Lloyd George.

A. J. BALFOUR (1848–1930). Conservative prime minister, 1902–5; resigns party leadership in 1911; first lord of the admiralty in the 1915 Coalition; foreign secretary in the Lloyd George Coalition. Signs the 'Balfour Declaration' of November 1917, which promises a homeland for Jews in Palestine.

DAVID BEATTY (1871–1936). Commander of the battle cruiser squadron of the British Grand Fleet at Jutland in 1916 – in which year he succeeds Jellicoe as commander of the fleet.

LEOPOLD Graf BERCHTOLD (1863–1942). Foreign minister of the Habsburg empire from 1912 to January 1915.

ANNIE BESANT (1847–1933). Active in socialist and secularist movements in England in the late nineteenth century. Settles in India, devoting herself to Indian political and social questions.

T. von BETHMANN HOLLWEG (1856–1921). German Conservative chancellor from 1909 until his resignation in July 1917.

P. BOSELLI (1838–1932). Veteran Italian politician. Forms Italian government in June 1916 which lasts until October 1917.

ARISTIDE BRIAND (1862–1932). Prominent French politician, holding many ministerial offices; prime minister, 1915–17.

A. A. BRUSILOV (1853–1926). Commander of Russian Eighth Army in Galicia in 1914–15. Commander of the South-West Russian front in March 1916. Launches summer offensive in that year. Holds supreme command, May–July 1917, under the Provisional government.

L. CADORNA (1850–1928). Italian general. Chief of staff, July 1914. Dismissed after Italian defeat at Caporetto, November 1917.

JOSEPH CAILLAUX (1863–1944). Prominent French prewar politician.

Advocate of Franco-German *rapprochement*. Involved in a distinctive variety of scandals.

ROBERT CECIL (1864–1958). Conservative MP from 1906. Foreign under-secretary, 1915–18 and minister of blockade, 1916–18, assistant foreign secretary, 1918–19; League of Nations enthusiast.

WINSTON CHURCHILL (1874–1965). First lord of the admiralty, 1911–15; resigns in wake of the failure of the Dardanelles attack in 1915; serves in the trenches; returns as minister of munitions in 1917.

GEORGES CLEMENCEAU (1841–1929). Prominent in late-nineteenth-century French politics. Prime minister, 1906–9. Critic of governments after 1914; prime minister and war minister in 1917.

F. CONRAD von HÖTZENDORF (1852–1925). Austrian general; commander of Habsburg forces against Russia in Galicia but dismissed in February 1917; successful commander on Italian front thereafter, though ultimate failure led to dismissal in July 1918.

A. DIAZ (1861–1928). Italian general. Succeeds Cadorna as chief of staff in November 1917.

M. ERZBERGER (1875–1921). Prominent German Catholic politician. Employed on wartime diplomatic missions. Supporter of the July 1917 Reichstag 'Peace Resolution'. Joins Prince Max of Baden's government in October 1918.

E. von FALKENHAYN (1861–1922). Prussian minister of war in 1913. Replaces Moltke after the battle of the Marne. Dismissed after the battle of Verdun (August 1916) but later has command in Romania, Palestine and elsewhere in the Near East.

FERDINAND, KING OF BULGARIA (1861–1948). Rules Bulgaria as prince from 1887 and as king from 1908–18. Frequently in conflict with Bulgarian politicians. Forced to abdicate.

JOHN FISHER (1841–1920). Second sea lord, 1902. First sea lord, 1904–10; promoter of the British Dreadnought programme. Retires in 1910 but returns as first sea lord in 1914; resigns over the Gallipoli campaign in 1915.

FRANZ FERDINAND (1863–1914). Austrian archduke, nephew of the emperor and heir to the Habsburg throne. His assassination precipitates the war.

FRANZ JOSEF (1830–1916). Emperor of Austria-Hungary; reigns 1848–1916.

L. FRANCHET D'ESPÉREY (1856–1942). French general who, after various Western front commands, leads the campaign out of Salonika which results in Bulgarian surrender in 1918.

JOHN FRENCH (1852–1925). Commander of the British Expeditionary Force, 1914–15; replaced by Haig in December 1915; thereafter commander of home forces; lord-lieutenant of Ireland, 1918–21.

J. GALLIÉNI (1849–1916). Military governor of Paris in August 1914; minister of war, October 1915–March 1916.

M. K. GANDHI (1869–1948). Indian lawyer, political and spiritual leader; active in South Africa before 1914; returns to India in 1915.

G. GIOLITTI (1842–1928). Veteran Italian politician; a great parliamentary manager who mismanages his wartime role.

I. L. GOREMYKIN (1839–1917). President of the Russian council of ministers, 1914–16.

EDWARD GREY (1862–1933). British Liberal foreign secretary, 1905–16; Coalition foreign secretary, 1915–16.

DOUGLAS HAIG (1861–1928). British general; commander-in-chief on the Western front, 1915–19.

MAURICE HANKEY (1877–1963). Secretary to the committee of imperial defence, 1912; secretary to the war council 1914–16 and the war cabinet, 1916–19.

HARDINGE of PENSHURST (1858–1944). Permanent under secretary at the foreign office, 1906–10; viceroy of India, 1910–16; returns to his old post in the foreign office, 1916–20.

ARTHUR HENDERSON (1863–1935). Leading Labour MP in 1914; joins the Coalition government in 1915 and Lloyd George's war cabinet in 1916; resigns in August 1917 in dispute about attendance at the proposed Stockholm peace conference.

G. von HERTLING (1843–1919). German Catholic politician; succeeds Michaelis as chancellor; resigns September 1918.

PAUL von HINDENBURG (1847–1934). German general, recalled from retirement in 1914 and commands German forces at the Masurian Lakes on the Eastern front; takes overall command in 1916 as chief of the general staff.

WILLIAM HUGHES (1862–1952). Australian Labour politician; prime minister in 1915; defeated in conscription referendum; forms his own party in 1916; prime minister for the remainder of the war.

JOHN JELLICOE (1859–1935). Commander of British Grand Fleet and fought battle of Jutland.

J. C. C. JOFFRE (1852–1931). French general; chief of staff, 1911; retired in 1916 and dispatched on mission to the United States.

MUSTAFA KEMAL (1880–1938). Turkish general, serves in Libyan and Balkan wars; divisional commander at Gallipoli; fights later in the Caucasus and Syria; founder of Turkish republic post war.

ALEXANDER KERENSKY (1881–1970). Russian lawyer and politician; justice minister in 1917 Provisional government, then war minister and, in July, prime minister; goes into exile after Bolshevik seizure of power.

H. H. KITCHENER (1850–1916). British general; commander-in-chief in India, 1902–9; secretary of state for war, 1914–16; drowned in May 1916.

L. G. KORNILOV (1870–1918). Russian general; succeeds Brusilov as commander-in-chief in July 1917; arrested after failure of his 'coup' in August 1917; after Bolshevik revolution escapes and founds anti-Bolshevik military units.

LANSDOWNE, Marquess of (1845–1927). British Conservative foreign secretary, 1900–5; Opposition leader in house of lords; serves without portfolio in Coalition government, 1915–16; author of 1917 letter urging possible negotiation of peace with Germany.

ANDREW BONAR LAW (1858–1923). British Conservative politician; succeeds Balfour as Opposition leader in 1911; colonial secretary in 1915 Coalition; chancellor of exchequer in 1916 Coalition.

T. E. LAWRENCE (1888–1935). Sent to Egypt in 1915 (having earlier worked in Mesopotamia) to work in military intelligence; helps to organize Feisal's revolt, advancing with him to Damascus in 1918.

V. I. LENIN (1870–1924). Russian revolutionary; in Switzerland in 1914; returns to Russia after the 1917 February revolution through good offices of the German government; architect of the Bolshevik revolution.

P. von LETTOW-VORBECK (1870–1964). Commander of German forces in German East Africa in 1914; though forced to concede much territory, he keeps fighting until the end of the war.

DAVID LLOYD GEORGE (1863–1945). British Liberal chancellor of the exchequer, 1908–15; minister of munitions, 1915–16; prime minister from December 1916.

E. LUDENDORFF (1865–1937). Captures Liège in 1914 but is then transferred to Eastern front as Hindenburg's chief of staff; chief quartermaster in August 1916 and Hindenburg's partner in overall direction of the German war effort.

A. von MACKENSEN (1849–1945). German commander of Austro-German forces in Galicia, 1915, in Serbia, 1915 and Macedonia in 1916.

L.-J. MALVY (1875–1949). French interior minister, 1914–17; sympathetic to negotiated peace and arrested, when Clemenceau became prime minister, for alleged contact with enemy agents.

C. MANGIN(1866–1925). French general; commander of Sixth Army during Nivelle offensive; demoted but then recalled for service in the last phase of the war.

ALFRED MILNER(1854–1925). British high commissioner in South Africa, 1897–1905; freelance politician; brought into his war cabinet by Lloyd George in 1916.

H. von MOLTKE (1848–1916). German general; succeeds Schlieffen as chief of the general staff in 1906; modified the Schlieffen plan but was forced to resign in autumn of 1914 in favour of Falkenhayn when the offensive did not succeed.

E. S. MONTAGU(1879–1924). British Liberal politician; chancellor of duchy of Lancaster, 1915–16; minister of munitions, 1916; secretary of state for India, 1917; author of proposals for increased Indian self-government.

BENITO MUSSOLINI (1883–1945). Italian socialist politician and journalist but expelled from the party for advocating Italian intervention in the war; joins Italian army and is injured.

NICHOLAS II (1868–1918). Tsar of Russia, 1894–1918; becomes his own commander-in-chief in 1915; abdicates in March 1917 and was shot by the Bolsheviks the following year.

R. G. NIVELLE (1856–1924). French general; steady advance through commands in the early years of the war; replaces Joffre as commander-in-chief in December 1916 but relieved of his command after the failure of the April 1917 offensive.

P. PAINLEVÉ (1863–1933). French mathematician and politician; minister of public instruction, 1915–16; minister of war, 1917; prime minister, 1917.

N. PAŠIĆ(1845–1926). Prime minister of Serbia, 1891–2, 1904–8, 1910–18; prominent in restoration of the Karadjordjević dynasty.

J. J. PERSHING (1860–1948). United States general; previous service in Cuba, Philippines and Mexico; commander of the American Expeditionary Force on the entry of the United States into the war.

P. PÉTAIN (1865–1951). French general; instructor, École de Guerre, 1901–10; service in the battle of the Marne, defender of Verdun; marshal of France, 1918; commander of French forces at the close of the war.

H. C. O. PLUMER (1857–1932). British general; service in Sudan and South African war; commander of the British Second Army, holding the Ypres salient; victor of Messines, 1917; again holds Ypres in 1918.

RAYMOND POINCARÉ (1860–1934). French politician and lawyer; president of the Republic, 1913–20.

O. von POTIOREK (1853–1933). Habsburg commander in invasion of Serbia in 1914; its failure leads to his dismissal at the end of 1914.

GAVRILO PRINCIP (1894–1918). Serbian assassin of Franz Ferdinand; dies in a Bohemian prison in 1918; body triumphantly returned to Sarajevo in 1920.

M. von PRITTWITZ (1848–1917). German general; defeats commander of German forces in initial Eastern front battles in August 1914; replaced by Hindenburg.

R. PUTNIK (1847–1917). Commander of Serbian forces in the Balkan wars and in the initial victories against the Habsburg forces in late 1914; director of the Serb retreat to the Adriatic; ill-health prevents any further war service.

GRIGORY RASPUTIN (c.1872–1916). Siberian mystic who gained great influence at the Russian court for his supposed ability to control the tsarevich Alexis's haemophilia; murdered in December 1916.

A. RIBOT (1842–1923). Veteran French politician; prime minister for the fifth time between March and September 1917.

WILLIAM ROBERTSON (1860–1933). British general; service in India and South Africa; chief of the general staff in 1915; resigns in February 1918.

A. SALANDRA (1853–1931). Prominent Italian politician and lawyer; prime minister, 1914–16; initially, advocate of Italian neutrality.

O. LIMAN von SANDERS (1855–1929). German soldier: leader of German military mission to Istanbul, 1913; plays prominent part in the Dardanelles campaign.

S. D. SAZONOV (1861–1927). Russian foreign minister, 1910–16, having previously served as a diplomat in London and at the Vatican.

R. SCHEER (1863–1928). German admiral; commander of the High Seas Fleet at Jutland.

A. von SCHLIEFFEN (1833–1913). German soldier: chief of the general staff, 1891–1906 and in this position devises the 'plan' which, modified, is the basis for German operations in 1914.

JAN SMUTS (1870–1950). South African (Afrikaner) soldier-politician; commander of British imperial forces in East Africa; joins the imperial war cabinet in London in 1917 and undertakes various diplomatic missions.

GUSTAV STRESEMANN (1878–1929). Prominent German National Liberal politician; advocate of annexationist policies and unconditional submarine warfare.

L. D. TROTSKY (1870–1940). Russian revolutionary in exile in France at outbreak of war; exiled to the United States: returns to Russia after the February revolution and plays a leading part in the October revolution; as commissar for foreign affairs, 1917–18, he conducts the negotiations with Germany at Brest-Litovsk; commissioner for war, 1918–25.

E. VENIZELOS (1864–1936). Prime minister of Greece from 1910 but in conflict with the royal household; resigns in 1915; backing from the Allies at Salonika assists his return to power in 1917 and promotes Greek intervention in the war.

R. VIVIANI (1863–1925). French journalist and politician; education minister, 1913–14; prime minister, June 1914–October 1915; justice minister, October 1915–September 1917.

WOODROW WILSON (1856–1924). Democratic president of the United States from 1913; takes the United States into the war on 6 April 1917.

Index

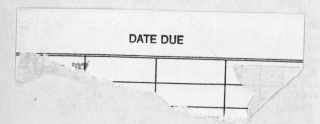

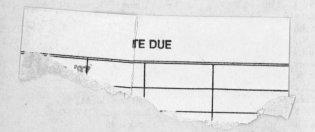